CRAZY MARY

I0139534

A R Gurney

BROADWAY PLAY PUBLISHING INC
New York
www.broadwayplaypublishing.com
info@broadwayplaypublishing.com

CRAZY MARY
© Copyright 2007 by A R Gurney

Cover photo by Joan Marcus
First printing: July 2007
I S B N: 978-0-88145-348-5
Book design: Marie Donovan
Word processing: Microsoft Word
Typographic controls: Ventura Publisher
Typeface: Palatino
Printed and bound in the U S A

CRAZY MARY was first produced at Playwrights
Horizons in New York City (Tim Sanford, Artistic
Director), opening on 3 June 2007 The cast and creative
contributors were as follows:

PEARL .... Myra Lucretia Taylor
SKIP ....Michael Esper
LYDIA .... Sigourney Weaver
JEROME .... Mitch Greenberg
MARY .... Kristine Nielsen

Director .... Jim Simpson
Set design ....John Lee Beatty
Costume design .... Claudia Brown
Lighting design ....Brian Aldous
Production stage manager ....Janet Takami
Assistant stage manager .... Cambra Overend

The play takes place in the "library" of a private psychiatric institution on the North Shore of Boston. The sanitarium was originally the sumptuous Peabody mansion, which was bought during the Depression and converted to its present use. Its library, with a massive and empty fireplace, oaken wainscoting, sconces, chandeliers, floor-to-ceiling bookcases, and occasional pieces of heavy furniture, still gives indications of the estate's former opulence. The ample book shelves, though now mostly empty, still display a few musty, bound sets of James Fennimore Cooper, Sir Walter Scott, and William Makepeace Thackeray, though they also now contain several rows of dog-eared paperbacks, along with stacks of old New Yorkers and National Geographic magazines. The contemporary world has also intruded with a stack of folding metal chairs for meetings tucked in a corner, along with a coffee hot plate, supported by packets of artificial creamer and paper cups. Several posters advertising recent cultural events are tacked to the walls, and there also is a bulletin board with various notices and announcements. Off in a corner is a battered upright piano, and a T V set on a moveable stand. The main entrance to this room is from a hallway through large wooden double doors, now modified with automatic closers and kick-stands if they are to be be kept open. Upstage, a small, private staircase leads to a landing and a closed door which provides a back entrance to the upstairs area of the house. Upstage also are French doors, through which one can get a sense of the grounds outside.

for Tim Sanford
and Playwrights Horizons

ACT ONE

(At rise:)

(Early spring. Afternoon. PEARL, *an African-American nurse in her forties, her profession indicated primarily by her thick-soled footwear and an institutional smock, enters with* SKIP *and* LYDIA *close behind her.* LYDIA *is a good looking, well-dressed, middle aged woman.* SKIP *is a college student, around twenty, somewhat scruffily dressed and carrying a back pack)*

PEARL: You can wait in here.

LYDIA: Thank you.

PEARL: We call this the library - which it was, actually, when this was a private mansion. You can tell by the book-shelves. And the woodwork along the walls.

LYDIA: Wainscoting.

PEARL: What?

LYDIA: That's called wainscoting.

SKIP: *(Low)* Mom.

PEARL: These fancy light fixtures came from back then, too.

LYDIA: I believe those are called sconces.

SKIP: Cool it, Mom.

LYDIA: I'm sorry, Skip, but I happen to know a thing or two about old houses. *(To* PEARL*)* I don't mean to correct you, but I work in real estate, back in Buffalo. Where we have plenty of old houses.

SKIP: And plenty on the market.

LYDIA: Poor old Buffalo.

PEARL: Here in Boston, we hold onto our history. There's a book about our old houses with a picture of this one. Before it became a sanitarium.

LYDIA: Interesting.

PEARL: It was set up for rich people. So they'd feel at home when they came here.

LYDIA: Ah yes.

PEARL: Rich people have mental problems too, you know.

LYDIA: *(Dryly)* Oh really.

PEARL: Money doesn't solve everything.

LYDIA: It sure can help.

PEARL: I'm with you there, ma'am. Oh yes indeed.

LYDIA: *(Going to a bookcase)* Skip, darling, look. Here's a leather-bound edition of the complete works of James Fennimore Cooper. Your grandfather had one just like it, in Cooperstown.

SKIP: *(To PEARL)* Do your patients use this room?

PEARL: Used to. When we had more live-ins. They'd read books here. Or watch the T V. Or play games. *(Indicating)* See? We've got Parcheesi, Chinese Checkers, and Clue here. Oh, and that piano. They say there was a famous poet from Harvard here, who used to play on that piano.

LYDIA: Skip here goes to Harvard.

SKIP: Here we go.

LYDIA: Junior year.

PEARL: Oh my.

SKIP: Forget it, Mom.

LYDIA: Well it's true.

SKIP: Big deal. Rah rah

PEARL: My brother-in-law's nephew goes to Harvard.

LYDIA: Good for him!

PEARL: Billy Johnson. He's very smart.

LYDIA: Do you know him, Skip? Billy Johnson?

SKIP: No I don't, Mom.

LYDIA: Well maybe you should. I imagine he's full of get-up-and-go. Skip will look him up, won't you, sweetie?

SKIP: *(Dryly)* Immediately. *(To* PEARL*)* So the patients won't be coming in here today?

PEARL: Not on weekends. Most health insurance won't pay for more than five working days.

LYDIA: Where do they go?

PEARL: Home, if they have one. Halfway houses. Sometimes to friends.

LYDIA: Poor souls.

PEARL: Yes well, you'll have this room to yourself. That's why the Doctor wanted to put you in here.

LYDIA: Does he know we've arrived?

PEARL: Oh yes. He's just finishing up his group.

LYDIA: His group?

PEARL: We do lots of groups here now. Outreach and groups. We have a chapter of A A meets here Tuesdays. And S C A meets every other Thursday.

LYDIA: S C A?

PEARL: Sexual Compulsives Anonymous.

SKIP: I should join that one.

PEARL: You need help there, honey?

LYDIA: *(To* PEARL*)* He does not. He just likes to tease.

PEARL: *(Laughing)* All right now... Woo.

LYDIA: Though I have to say he likes the ladies.

PEARL: I'll bet the ladies like him, Harvard and all.

LYDIA: Absolutely. Right, Skip?

SKIP: Wrong, Mom.

LYDIA: *(To* PEARL*)* He's just being modest. He lives with this wonderful girl. She's to die for, isn't she, Skip?

SKIP: *(Dryly)* Oh sure, Mom. You bet.

LYDIA: *(Looking at her watch)* I wonder if there's any way of hurrying things along. I have a plane to catch.

PEARL: I'll go check. *(She starts out, stops.)* Help yourselves to coffee. I made it fresh. *(She goes.)*

SKIP: *(Tossing his backpack somewhere, going to coffee stand)* Want some?

LYDIA: No thanks.

SKIP: *(Helping himself)* I could use a fix.

LYDIA: I don't know why doctors can't be on time for their appointments like everyone else in the world. You set a specific date and time, and then it's wait, wait, wait. I find it infuriating.

SKIP: Tell you one thing. I'm feeling creepier by the minute.

LYDIA: So am I, but this has got to be done.

SKIP: Why?

LYDIA: Why? Because it's my family responsibility, that's why. And who knows? Some day it may be yours.

SKIP: How come you lied?

LYDIA: I don't know what you're talking about.

SKIP: That stuff about catching a plane.

LYDIA: I do have to catch one.

SKIP: Tomorrow *morning*, Mom. Remember? You're taking Becky and me to dinner tonight.

LYDIA: I adore Becky. I like her so much more than those empty-headed preppy types you used to squire around.

SKIP: Don't change the subject. You lied.

LYDIA: I exaggerated, Skipper, because I believe in moving things along. Frankly, I felt that woman was stalling.

SKIP: I'll bet "that woman" is a registered nurse, Mother.

LYDIA: Whatever she is, she was stalling. Herding us into this back room. Plying us with coffee. They're avoiding the issue. I feel it in my bones.

SKIP: Oh come on.

LYDIA: It's part of a pattern, Skip. They didn't answer my letter. When I called, they put me on hold. I sat on the phone for ten minutes, long distance, listening to that hideous tune from *Doctor Zhivago*.

SKIP: You got your appointment, didn't you?

LYDIA: Finally. After an official letter from our lawyer.

SKIP: You're paranoid, Mom.

LYDIA: We'll see, we'll see. There may be more going on here than meets the—

SKIP: *(Looking out through the doorway)* Hold it.
He's coming.

*(JEROME enters, in shirtsleeves. He carries a stack of old
and dusty manila folders)*

JEROME: Howdy, howdy, howdy.. *(Holding out his hand)*

LYDIA: *(Shaking it)* Doctor.

JEROME: Jerome, please. "Doctor" doesn't work well for
me.

LYDIA: Surely you have your M D?

JEROME: Plus a master's in pharmacology. And another
in hospital administration. But I prefer first names.
It puts us more on an equal footing.

LYDIA: I suppose that makes me Lydia.

JEROME: Good. Now I won't have to pronounce your
last name, Lydia.

LYDIA: Nobody can. It's Polish. But now I'm divorced,
I plan to change it back.

SKIP: Hey! Since when?

LYDIA: Since your dear father's most recent check
bounced higher than the moon. *(To JEROME, indicating)*
My son Skip. He's the first male in my family not to be
named after his father.... He got to skip all that Junior
stuff because I married one Mirek Tobijasiewicz. The
only Junior he is, is a junior at Harvard.

JEROME: *(Shaking hands)* I'm impressed.

SKIP: That's why she squeezed that in.

LYDIA: Because I'm proud of you, darling.. *(Arm around
SKIP; to JEROME)* This boy is my strength and salvation....

SKIP: *(Breaking away; to JEROME)* Wait till she hears my
latest my grade point average.

LYDIA: Nonsense. *(To* JEROME*)* He wants to go on to the Harvard Business School

SKIP: Jerome doesn't care about my educational plans, Mom.

LYDIA: Well I care. Very much. And I'm willing to work my tail off to pay for them.

JEROME: *(Indicating)* Speaking of our tails, shall we sit down?

LYDIA: *(Sitting)* Thank you.

JEROME: Anyone like coffee?

LYDIA: Not me, thanks.

SKIP: I'll have a little more.

JEROME: Help yourself.

LYDIA: *(To* JEROME*)* I assume you've noticed that this generation seems to be o.d.-ing regularly on caffeine. And when they're not doing that, they suck on bottles of water. I suppose you'll say it's a Freudian thing.

SKIP: *(As he fixes his coffee)* Better coffee than booze, Mom. Better Starbucks than the Saturn Club bar.

LYDIA: *(To* JEROME*)* He thinks everyone in my family is an alcoholic.

SKIP: Oh God no. Just your father. And your father's sister. And your brother and—

LYDIA: That's enough, sweetheart.

SKIP: It's more than enough

LYDIA: *(To* JEROME*)* We suddenly seem to be airing our dirty laundry in front of you.

JEROME: It's my therapeutic personality. My wife says I bring out the worst in people. .

LYDIA: Be careful, Skipper. Or Jerome here will send us a bill.

JEROME: Not in your case. You're already paying plenty.

LYDIA: Which reminds me, let's get down to business.

JEROME: All right. *(Takes an official looking letter from his top folder)* Shall we start with this letter from your lawyer? He indicates that you want to discuss the condition of a patient here, namely our dear Mary...

LYDIA: That's it

JEROME: And you, he says here, are her next of kin.

LYDIA: I am now. My father was, but he died recently.

JEROME: I'm sorry.

LYDIA: He left me in charge.

SKIP: Though he left her nothing else.

LYDIA: Please, Skip.

JEROME: May I ask how you and Mary are related?

LYDIA: My great-grandfather was Mary's grandfather. My father's father was her father's brother.

JEROME: Say that again.

SKIP: She's my mother's second cousin.

LYDIA: Once removed.

SKIP: Totally removed, if you ask me.

LYDIA: We didn't ask you, Skip dear.

JEROME: This letter inquires about the patient's mental condition and goes on to request... *(Reads from letter)* ..."a more specific accounting of the trust fund provided for her support".

LYDIA: Because I'm now the trustee.

JEROME: You and the Bank of Boston.

LYDIA: The point is, Mary was the only "issue" on that branch of the family, and since she had no children, her estate reverted back up the line, and came on down to my father, and now me.

JEROME: *(Referring to letter)* "Per stirpes", it says here.

LYDIA: That means "through the roots". This whole situation simply fell into my lap, so here we are, to find out what's what.

JEROME: Of course

LYDIA: I knew her a little, you know.

JEROME: You knew our Mary?

LYDIA: Way back when. Our great grandfather had this place on the lake in Cooperstown, and we all visited in the summer.

JEROME: *(Taking out a pencil)* Mind if I write this down?

LYDIA: Not at all.

JEROME: Feel free to keep talking as I do. *(He writes in the most current folder.)*

LYDIA I remember he built this special playhouse for his grandchildren, and I played there with Mary. She was a little older than I was but—oh, and this should interest you. We all called her Crazy Mary.

JEROME: *(As he writes)* Do you remember why?

LYDIA: I guess we thought she was kind of nutty. She'd have these...ups and downs. Sometimes you might say she was higher than a kite.

JEROME: Go on.

LYDIA: And sometimes just the reverse.

JEROME: She'd close down?

LYDIA: Totally. Knock, knock. Who's there? Nobody home.

JEROME: Mmm.

LYDIA: Of course, my great-grandfather had died by then, but my grandfather held onto the place till *he* died. Then we all went our separate ways, and kind of lost track of Mary.

JEROME: *(Opening another old folder)* According to our records, she was admitted here in 1973. *(He blows some dust off the folder)*

SKIP: *(Looking up from his book)* 1973? Vietnam and Watergate.

LYDIA: The whole country was in a turmoil, wasn't it?

JEROME: Certainly Mary was, when they committed her. *(Reads)* I notice here that her first psychiatrist still uses the quaint old term, "Nervous breakdown". *(To* LYDIA*)* Which was the genteel way of describing any kind of psychological disorder.

SKIP: 1973! Whoa! That means she's been here for...what? Over thirty years!

JEROME: Looks that way.

SKIP: That's a long time to be imprisoned in the Bastille.

JEROME: Ah well, what with the new drugs and a different attitude toward mental illness, people are released from the Bastille pretty regularly these days. How does Dickens describe it in *A Tale of Two Cities*?

LYDIA: Haven't the foggiest.

SKIP: "Recalled to life."

JEROME: That's it.

LYDIA: *(To* JEROME*)* See? Harvard.

JEROME: More and more patients are being "recalled to life".

LYDIA: But not Mary?

JEROME: Ah no. But there's always hope. We're always trying new therapies.

LYDIA: Really? Why weren't we told that?

JEROME: I believe you were. *(Thumbing through folders)* I notice here that my several predecessors submitted annual reports on Mary's condition to your law firm in Buffalo. But no one wrote back. *(Holding up a hand-written note from a folder)* For example, here's a note to our staff here from one Doctor Silverman who took over in the eighties. He says... *(Reads)* "No response from Buffalo. It's like shouting down a well." *(Thumbing through folders, blowing off the dust)* Anyway, by 1995, two psychiatrists later, we seem to have stopped writing.

LYDIA: Seems to me there's been considerable negligence around here.

JEROME: Here and elsewhere, dear lady. Here and elsewhere.

SKIP: Touché.

JEROME: And I suppose poor Mary fell between the cracks.

LYDIA: On her side of the family, there was no one left. On our side, we didn't know...

SKIP: Or didn't care.

LYDIA: Oh Skip, really! How many people in the world keep close tabs on their second cousins?

SKIP: This is the way our family has always dealt with uncomfortable issues, Jerome. We toss money at it, if

we have any. Then we turn our backs, and walk away.
Wasn't there, didn't happen. Period. End of story.

LYDIA: Oh honestly.

SKIP: Like my Dad. Who was dropped like a hot potato.

LYDIA: Because he wouldn't lift a finger.

SKIP: Lift a finger? *(To* JEROME*)* He only played the
bassoon in the Buffalo Philharmonic Orchestra. Which
takes a considerable amount of expert finger-lifting.

LYDIA: He did nothing else, Skip.

SKIP: Except shift to the tenor sax and become one of
great jazz soloists in the Western New York area.

LYDIA: *(To* JEROME*)* And come home at three in the
morning ....

SKIP: *(To* JEROME*)* Until he was summarily locked out.

LYDIA: *(To* JEROME*)* Talk about dirty laundry. I suppose
you're writing all this down.

JEROME: Would you prefer I didn't?

LYDIA: Oh well, you're the Doctor.

JEROME: I keep reminding myself of that.

SKIP: Tell us more about Mary.

LYDIA: Yes, exactly. Let's get back on track here.
Where do you keep her?

JEROME: *(Indicating staircase and door)* She's one of our
last in-house patients. She has what was once the
master bedroom. It's a large, light room, with its own
bath and a radio, which she turns on occasionally.
And a television set which she doesn't. And of course,
she lives under careful supervision night and day.

LYDIA: Do you ever let her out?

JEROME: On the hospital grounds, of course. Beyond that, no.

LYDIA: Why not? If everyone else around here is being recalled to...recalled to whatever.

SKIP: *Life*, Mom. Life's the word.

LYDIA: *(To* JEROME*)* So why doesn't she go farther?

JEROME: I believe she's afraid she'd be overwhelmed.

LYDIA: She's that far gone?

JEROME: Not gone, really. Just not quite here.

LYDIA: What does she do with her days?

JEROME: Depends on the day.

LYDIA: Does she read, for example?

JEROME: Not much.

LYDIA: Does she connect with other patients?

JEROME: She's mostly afraid to.

LYDIA: Afraid of what?

JEROME: Being rejected. Abandoned. Someone must have let her down, once upon a time.

LYDIA: So she doesn't see anyone?

JEROME: She sees Pearl, who showed you in here. Mary connects strongly with her. And visa versa.

LYDIA: Then she talks, at least.

JEROME: Occasionally.

LYDIA: Does she make sense?

JEROME: Depends on the occasion.

LYDIA: So she primarily just...sits around?.

JEROME: Sits. Walks around. *(Looking off)* Sometimes, on a good day, she likes to climb the back stairs to the East wing, where the maids' rooms used to be. One of them has a good view, all the way to Boston. So she goes up there and looks out.

LYDIA: It all sounds terribly, terribly sad.

JEROME: Not always. Sometimes she sings. She's got a sweet voice.

LYDIA: I remember that, from Cooperstown. We'd sing around the piano. What does she sing?

JEROME: I haven't noticed any particular song. She's a difficult one, our Mary. *(Indicating folders)* Look at all the differing opinions about her. Write-up after write-up, year after year, all over the map...

LYDIA: Is there a name for her condition?

JEROME: *(Consulting a folder)* I notice that here's where she was diagnosed as schizophrenic. That's obviously wrong. But most of these designations aren't much use these days. Every case is so different. And every doctor, too, I should add. "Bi-polar" is the current jargon. But I'm hardly satisfied with it.

LYDIA: How about some of the new drugs?

JEROME: Ah, well. I'm trying a whole new protocol. *(Indicating newest folder)* One of the medications is so new I haven't yet learned how to pronounce it.

LYDIA: And?

JEROME: I sense a tiny glimmer. Pearl does, too. Or thinks she does.

LYDIA: Hmmm. Well. We should talk about the money thing.

SKIP: Money, money, money.

LYDIA: As a trustee, Skip, I should at least be aware of how much is involved. The bank statements are almost totally incomprehensible.

JEROME: I can tell you it's a sizeable trust.

LYDIA: I imagine so. Knowing my great-grandfather.

SKIP: Those guys cleaned up. No income tax. No unions. No social conscience.

LYDIA: All I know is that Mary inherited everything on her side.

SKIP: While we were pissing away everything on ours.

LYDIA: *(To* SKIP*)* I would really and truly appreciate a few less snide comments from the peanut gallery, thank you very much.

SKIP: I can't help it , Mom. I'm a compulsive wise guy.

LYDIA: It certainly seems that way today. *(To* JEROME*)* Can you tell me how you spend Mary's money?

JEROME: *(Again consulting folders)* Ah well. I'm going to be frank here.

LYDIA: I should hope so.

JEROME: Since Mary's needs are somewhat limited, we occasionally use portions of her income elsewhere.

LYDIA: Elsewhere?

JEROME: On patients who otherwise couldn't afford any therapy at all. And on several outreach programs in the inner city.

LYDIA: What you're saying is you're spending my family's money, but not on Mary.

JEROME: Not only on Mary.

SKIP: What's wrong with that? There's no point in letting it just pile up.

LYDIA: Oh really, Skip? You like the idea of throwing money around? Even though, as a scholarship student at Harvard, you spend half your evenings stacking trays in the cafeterias?

SKIP: It won't kill me.

LYDIA: Well it's killing me, my friend. Do you think I enjoy driving around Buffalo, trying to sell old houses to people who can't appreciate them, without a nickel of support from you-know-who? *(To* JEROME*)* We were speaking of money.

JEROME: We were indeed. And if you prefer we confine it to Mary, we'll have to oblige.

LYDIA: I suppose it depends on Mary, doesn't it? How she is.

JEROME: I suppose it does.

LYDIA: *(Indicating staircase)* So: may we see her?

JEROME: Bad idea.

LYDIA: Why so?

JEROME: She doesn't want to see you.

LYDIA: How do you know that?

JEROME: Because I brought it up to her after I got your letter. And mentioned it again when you said you were coming. She said No.

LYDIA: Just No.

JEROME: No the first time. The second time she simply didn't respond.

LYDIA: Oh dear.

JEROME: Well, you can understand that. After thirty odd years? To confront a couple of strangers? I don't dare take the risk.

LYDIA: You mean she's dangerous?

SKIP: He means we are, Mom

LYDIA: We're her family, for God's sake!

SKIP: That's why we're dangerous.

LYDIA: Skip, I am fast losing patience. *(To* JEROME*)* Couldn't we just take a peek? Through a crack in the door or something?

SKIP: *(To* JEROME*)* My mother thinks she's at the Buffalo zoo.

JEROME: We never allow visitors above the first floor.

LYDIA: Couldn't you bring her down? Just for a minute?

JEROME: Perhaps some other time.

LYDIA: You seem to think I live right around the corner.

JEROME: Surely you'll be back.

LYDIA: Who knows when.

SKIP: When I flunk out of Harvard. To pick up my stuff.

LYDIA: Skip...

JEROME: Give us a few weeks to prepare her. Could you do that?

LYDIA: I could not, Jerome. I can't commute to Boston every other minute. So I'd very much like to see my own cousin while I'm here...

JEROME: I'll have to think about this.

LYDIA: *(To* JEROME*)* Do you know what my lawyer thinks?

SKIP: Chill, Mom. Chill out.

JEROME: What does your lawyer think, Lydia?

LYDIA: He thinks that in view of the consistent lack of information on Mary, as well as those indecipherable statements from the Bank of Boston...

SKIP: Get ready to duck, Jerome. Here it comes...

LYDIA: ...my lawyer thinks that, for all we know, our dear Crazy Mary may have been dead and buried for some time, while you people continue to make use of her considerable income.

JEROME: That's what your lawyer thinks?

SKIP: He picked up that plot point from Law and Order...

JEROME: Do you agree with your lawyer, Lydia?

LYDIA: I do think I have the right to a short glimpse of my own cousin, since she is now very much my personal responsibility.

JEROME: But Pearl said you have a plane to catch.

LYDIA: I'd be willing to forego that flight till tomorrow morning.

SKIP: *(Wryly)* Oh wow, Mom! That's big of you!

(JEROME crosses to a house phone on the wall.)

JEROME *(On phone)* Pearl! Would you come here a minute , please?

(A short, silent wait. [Late audience members can be seated at this point.] PEARL appears in the doorway)

PEARL: *(To others, with a wink)* Her Master's voice.

JEROME: *(Quietly)* Pearl, do you think we could get Mary ready to see visitors?

LYDIA: To see her family.

PEARL: Mary? My Mary?

JEROME: I'll come up and give you a hand with her.

PEARL: You serious?

JEROME: I'm afraid I have to be.

PEARL: Oh my poor baby. *(She crosses to staircase, goes up, and out)*

JEROME: *(Following* PEARL; *turning at top of stairs)*
This may take a little time *(He goes out, losing the door behind him.)*

(Pause) SKIP *(To* LYDIA*)* Nice going.

LYDIA: You think I went overboard?

SKIP: *(Sarcastically)* Oh no, no, no.

LYDIA: I had to do it. We owe it to Mary. It's our family responsibility to follow through on the poor thing.

SKIP: "Thing," Mom? "Thing"?

LYDIA: O K, person. I couldn't live with myself if I shuffled back to Buffalo without knowing more about what's going on. If she's well taken care of, fine. If she's not, we'll make sure that she is. If it takes her entire income to make her comfortable, fair enough, that's life. But if she's dead...

SKIP: Oh come on...

LYDIA: There could easily be some hanky-panky going on here, Skip.

SKIP: I doubt it very much.

LYDIA: Well if there is, the money's come to us, and Lord knows we can use it.

SKIP: For...?

LYDIA: For you, my friend.

SKIP: I don't want it or need it.

LYDIA: You need it desperately, Skip, whether you know it or not. I frankly think you'd be doing a lot better at Harvard if you didn't have all those student jobs.

SKIP: The jobs aren't the problem.

LYDIA: They don't give you time to study.

SKIP: How the hell would you know?

LYDIA: Becky told me. She telephoned specially.

SKIP: You know what? That kind of pisses me off. Her calling you that way.

LYDIA: You're lucky to have her. She works hard, she organizes her life. She said last year she helped you with a term paper.

SKIP: She practically wrote the thing.

LYDIA: There you are. I keep telling you, sweetheart, stick with the Jews.

SKIP: Oh I get it now. You like her because she's Jewish.

LYDIA: What's wrong with that? The Jews know who they are and where they're going. As opposed to some people around here.

SKIP: *(Miming being stabbed in the gut)* Ooh. Ouch. Help.

LYDIA: I specifically asked Becky if your scholarship jobs dragged you down. She said that was a definite possibility.

SKIP: She should have said that I'm just not interested.

LYDIA: What? What do I hear? Not interested? Not interested in graduating from the finest university in the country? When people all over the world would give their eye-teeth just to get near the place?

SKIP: How do you make yourself interested, Mom? Answer me that. How do you get yourself to want? It all seems so...old hat.

LYDIA: Old hat? You got that expression from me, old hat.

SKIP: I got too much from you.

LYDIA: You didn't get the habit of sitting on the sidelines and being disagreeable. That's not my solution, I can tell you that.

SKIP: What's your solution, Mom?

LYDIA: My solution is to take a deep breath, tighten your grip, and make a concerted effort to run with the ball.

SKIP: Just like that, huh?

LYDIA: Skip, I promise you life will get easier in business school....

SKIP: I don't want to go to business school

LYDIA: Medical school, then. Law school. You name it. You're destined to do well in life, darling. That I know. You're smart, you're a lovely athlete, you were Vice President of your class at Andover. You're going to put us back on the map, darling. I feel it in my bones.

SKIP: Talk about pressure.

LYDIA: Well I'm sorry, but I happen to believe in you. And I also happen to believe that money helps, dear heart. It helps you live, it helps you breathe. When Becky's family invited you along on that trip to Mexico last Christmas, could you go? You could not. Because you didn't have the money to pull your own weight.

SKIP: *(Dryly)* Oh? Was that the reason?

LYDIA: It was, because you're...well, you're a gentleman, frankly, whether you know it or not. And being one takes money. And I'll tell you something else. I could use some myself. Just once in my life, before I die, I'd like to drive a decent car, and own a decent refrigerator, and travel first-class to Europe the way my parents did, every other year.

SKIP: I'll be off your back soon, Mom, one way or another. I swear.

LYDIA: Will you? Then how come you turned down that paid internship at Goldman Sachs this summer?

SKIP: Because I already have a job this summer.

LYDIA: Mowing people's lawns?

SKIP: Working on people's gardens. You should see the vegetable garden I set up for the Watsons last summer.

LYDIA: Are you now saying you want to be a farmer?

SKIP: My great-grandfather was a farmer. That was a farm he had in Cooperstown.

LYDIA: "Farm" is just an expression. They all did that.

SKIP: I've checked the old photo albums, Mom They had a major vegetable garden. And cows. And chickens. .

LYDIA: With umpteen people to take care of them.

SKIP: Still, it looks like a wonderful way to live.

LYDIA: In the summer, period.

SKIP: I can see doing it all year round.

LYDIA: I am absolutely amazed! I'm not sure I know you at all.

(JEROME *comes in.*)

JEROME: Get ready, please.

LYDIA: She's coming?

JEROME: Pearl's got her to the top of the stairs.

LYDIA: What should we...do?

JEROME: Do? Nothing. Be calm. Speak quietly. Behave as if this were the most ordinary thing in the world.

SKIP: Which it isn't.

JEROME: You're right about that one. (*He goes out into the hall, looks off*) And lo and behold.

(A moment. Then PEARL *comes on, leading* MARY, *looking wide-eyed and frightened. She has grayish hair, which has been hastily combed into place and held with a pathetic little ribbon . She wears an institutional gown under a scruffy bathrobe and shoddy slippers.)*

PEARL: *(Gently, holding* MARY's *arm, leading her downstairs)* Here's my baby. Here's my girl.

JEROME: Will you greet your visitors, Mary?

LYDIA: *(To* MARY*)* We're your family, Mary...

*(*MARY *doesn't look or respond)*

PEARL: Look, Mary. See the nice lady and the nice young man. *(To* LYDIA*)* What relation are you again?

LYDIA: Cousins.

PEARL: Your cousins have come visiting, Mary honey. *(To* LYDIA*)* Today's not one of her talking days. *(To* MARY*)* Right, Mary, child? You're not saying a word. *(To* LYDIA *and* SKIP*)* She's a little cranky because she was listening to the opera. She loves the opera on Saturday afternoons.

JEROME: *(To* PEARL*)* Have her sit down. *(Takes a chair from somewhere, sets it up so that* MARY *will be facing* LYDIA *and* SKIP *when she sits)* Here you are, Mary. Here's a chair for you....

PEARL: Want to sit here, honey? So your cousins can see you?

*(*MARY *sits.* PEARL *stands beside her, fixing her hair)*

PEARL: My, don't we look pretty today.

LYDIA: *(To* JEROME*)* May we talk to her?

JEROME: You can try.

LYDIA: *(Awkwardly)* Remember me, Mary? *(Nothing)* I'm Lydia. *(Nothing)* Remember the playhouse in the

summer at Cooperstown? *(Nothing)* And the pony?
(To others) My grandfather got us a pony. *(To* MARY*)*
What was the pony's name, Mary? Neddy! Remember
Neddy the pony? And the pony cart? *(To others)*
They'd hitch this pony to a cart and let us drive him
around. *(To* MARY*)* Remember that, Mary? *(To* JEROME*)*
I'm not getting through.

JEROME: It's hard to tell.

LYDIA: How about the croquet games, Mary?
Remember those?

JEROME: Say, do you mind if I write this down?

LYDIA: What's to write?

JEROME: The whole thing. It thickens the stew.

SKIP: On T V, they call it the back story.

JEROME: Whatever it is, it's fascinating.

LYDIA: *(To* PEARL*)* I can't get a reaction.

PEARL: She's taking it well, though. *(To* MARY*)* Aren't
you, dear? You're taking it well. *(To others)* I was scared
she might start screaming. But she's taking it very well.

JEROME: Good point, Pearl. *(He writes.)*

*(*MARY *vaguely looks around.)*

PEARL: She's remembering the room.

LYDIA: She's been here before?

PEARL: Oh yes. I bring her down sometimes. We play
a nice game of Chinese Checkers, don't we, Mary? *(To*
LYDIA*)* Or she looks through the magazines. *(To* MARY*)*
You like *The New Yorker*, don't you, honey? *(To others)*
She likes the ads in *The New Yorker* magazine.. *(Brings
a* New Yorker *to* MARY*)* Remember looking at this one,
Mary?

LYDIA: Do you remember Freulein, Mary? *(To others)* She had this German nurse. We all had to call her Freulein. *(To MARY)* Remember, Mary? *(To others)* When Mary was naughty, Freulein used to slap her face. *(To MARY)* Remember that, Mary? Ouch! And in croquet, you always had to have the red ball... Oh, and swimming in Glimmerglass lake? The raft? Remember when we were allowed to swim out to the raft? *(To others)* Hopeless.

JEROME: You'd be surprised. Sometimes I'll have a session with her and get nothing at all, and then next time she'll open up.

PEARL: *(Fixing MARY's hair)* Isn't she pretty, though?

JEROME: I read in one of her earlier files that she was very beautiful.

LYDIA: She was. I was quite jealous. *(To MARY)* I was jealous of you, Mary. To me, you were the Queen Bee. You ruled the roost.

JEROME: What are your thoughts here, Skip?

SKIP: Me? Oh I'm just an innocent bystander.

(MARY might glance at him for a moment)

LYDIA: I wish there were something we could... *(Thinking)* Music! How about music? *(To JEROME)* You said she liked music.

PEARL: Oh my, she surely does. She likes the classical music on her radio. She hears it every morning. And the opera. She always gets quiet for that.

LYDIA: Does she understand what's going on?

PEARL: Oh I think so. But she don't like those intermissions when the folks start showing how smart they are.

SKIP: I'm with her on that one.

(Again MARY *might glance at him)*

LYDIA: Skipper plays the piano.

SKIP: I do not.

LYDIA: You play, Skip. You just don't practice enough....
(To others) He plays by ear. When we had our piano
in Buffalo, Skip would sometimes come down in the
middle of the night and play his heart out. He's got a
love of music.

SKIP: My father's love of music.

LYDIA: Play something for her, Skip. Just to see.

SKIP: What'll I play?

LYDIA: Something she might know. Some older song.

PEARL: Sometimes she sings a little.

LYDIA: What does she sing? Do you know any of the
songs?

PEARL: She sings a song about the sunshine.

SKIP: "You are my Sunshine"?

PEARL: There you go.

LYDIA: Of course. We used to sing that around the
piano in Cooperstown. Try playing it, Skip.

SKIP: I don't know it.

LYDIA: You can pick it out. *(To* JEROME *and* PEARL*)*
This boy used to play anything we asked. When we'd
go visit my father, he'd say, "Play cocktail music for us,
Skipper". And Skip would sit right down and play
Irving Berlin and Cole Porter. Of course now it's like
pulling teeth. *(To* SKIP*)* Just give it a try, Skip. Will you
do that for your mother, please?

PEARL: Do it for Mary. Do it for my honey here.

(SKIP *reluctantly crosses to the piano, sit down, plays a chord or two*)

SKIP: This instrument is totally out of tune.

JEROME: I'm sure.

(SKIP *starts playing, slowly and carefully*)

LYDIA: (*Starting to sing along*)
You are my sunshine...my only sunshine...

(*To* MARY, *as* SKIP *continues to play*)

LYDIA: Remember, Mary? After supper? In Cooperstown?

(*Still nothing from* MARY)

SKIP: (*Singing along*)
You make me happy...when skies are gray...
You'll never know, dear, how much I love you,
Please don't take my sunshine away.

(*He finishes with a chord.* MARY *slightly turns her head in his direction as if she has noticed he's stopped*)

PEARL: Did you see that?

JEROME: See what?

PEARL: She noticed. She turned her head.

JEROME: I didn't see it.

LYDIA: Neither did I.

PEARL: She liked the song, didn't you, Mary?

(SKIP *leaves the piano. He crosses in front of* MARY. *She follows him briefly with her eyes.*)

LYDIA: (*Getting up*) Well. I suppose we should go.

JEROME: Yes. Your plane.

SKIP: Right. You never know what time it might take off.

LYDIA: Let's go, Skip.

JEROME: You might tell your lawyer you've seen our Mary, Lydia.

LYDIA: I intend to.

JEROME: And I hope you'll add that she's very much alive, and not some substitute we trotted out for the occasion.

LYDIA: I'll have to go on faith on that one.

SKIP: If faith is good enough for our current president, it's good enough for my mother.

LYDIA: *(To* JEROME*)* He hates Bush.

SKIP: Wrong, Mom. I identify with the guy. He's a kid from Andover in the wrong slot at the wrong time, so he's messing up, just like me.

JEROME: As for the money, Lydia ...

LYDIA: Our lawyer will work with the bank on that.

JEROME: It's Mary's money, of course.

LYDIA: It's family money. And I'm also aware that there's more than one way to skin a cat.

JEROME: I don't believe in skinning cats.

LYDIA: This is becoming a silly conversation.... Come on, Skip. *(She goes out)*

SKIP: *(Shaking hands)* Thanks, Jerome.

JEROME: I'd better see your mother to the door.

SKIP: Yes, you'd better. Or I'll hear about it later.

*(*JEROME *follows* LYDIA *out.)*

SKIP: Thanks, Pearl.

PEARL: You're welcome, hon.

*(*SKIP *goes.)*

*(*PEARL *helps* MARY *up from her chair.)*

PEARL: Let's go, gal. Back to *Lucy Lammermoor*...

*(*SKIP *returns.)*

SKIP: Forgot my back pack... Loaded with Harvard stuff. *(Looks around)* Think Freud would have something to say about that, Pearl?

PEARL: I'm not saying a word.

SKIP: *(Finds his bag. He goes to* MARY *who is by now on the landing of the back staircase)* Goodbye, Mary. *(He starts out again.)*

MARY: *(Calling after him)* Come back.

*(*SKIP *stops, turns and looks at her, then at* PEARL*.)*

PEARL: She said, "come back".

SKIP: I will.

PEARL: Promise her. She likes promises.

SKIP: *(To* MARY*)* I promise, Mary. *(He goes)*

PEARL: Why, Mary! You like that boy, don't you, honey?

*(*MARY *nods.)*

PEARL: You go, girl!

*(*PEARL *leads* MARY *out, blackout)*

(Possibly several bars of Lucia's mad scene from the opera)

(A week later. The reception room is now empty. Then PEARL *enters through the French doors carrying a vase of cut daffodils. She places them somewhere prominent, and begins to arrange them.* JEROME *comes in. He now wears a jacket and has his folders with him)*

JEROME: Daffodils!

PEARL: There's whole patches growing over by the parking lot.

JEROME: That's where they had the old gardens.

PEARL: Daffodils don't give up.

JEROME: They certainly add a festive note.

PEARL: *(Checking watch)* Skip better show, after all this.

JEROME: *(Checking his watch)* I told him to come right on back when he gets here.

PEARL: Should we have Mary waiting for him, or him waiting for Mary?

JEROME: How about the latter? He's an admirer, making a call. And she's the lady of the house, coming downstairs to see who it is.

PEARL: I already told her to pretend it's a big surprise.

JEROME: Women are good at that.

PEARL: I hope Mary is.

JEROME: You never know, with Mary.

PEARL: What does the mama say about all this?

JEROME: I haven't told her.

PEARL: What?

JEROME: Skip asked me not to.

PEARL: She should know.

JEROME: Sooner or later.

PEARL: You went for later.

JEROME: Right.

PEARL: Why? Scared she might close it down?

JEROME: I wanted to see what would happen without her.

PEARL: You could write a book about this.

JEROME: Tell you a secret, Pearl. *(Displaying a small spiral notebook)* I already am.

PEARL: You're always writing books.

JEROME: Always trying. This is the first that might go somewhere.

PEARL: I'm rooting for you.

JEROME: Thanks... So: tell me about our prom queen... Did we solve the clothes problem?

PEARL: Finally. She wouldn't wear any of her hospital stuff, and we didn't keep any of her own things, and when I put her in a dress left by old Mrs Fenton, Mary looked in the mirror and started to cry.

JEROME: Sounds like my daughter getting ready for high school.

PEARL: Tell me about it... Finally I found a party dress left over from one of those plays the patients used to put on.

JEROME: She went for it?

PEARL: Only after I made some alterations.

JEROME: You're a prize, Pearl.

PEARL: She didn't like her hair, though.

JEROME: What woman does?

PEARL: We had to make a special trip to the hairdresser's. And last night she wore curlers to bed.

JEROME: No!

PEARL: Wouldn't go to sleep till I went and got curlers from the C V S.

JEROME: Keep the receipts, Pearl. You'll be reimbursed.

PEARL: I have to say this makes me a little nervous.

JEROME: Nervous?

PEARL: Messing around with Mary this way.

JEROME: Look at it as therapy, Pearl.

PEARL: Some therapy.

JEROME: She's better, isn't she? Now she's knows he's coming.

PEARL: She still shuts down some. Or starts repeating.

JEROME: But generally, it's an improvement.

PEARL: Oh yes.

JEROME: And remember. She asked for this. On her own. We're only doing what the patient asked for.

PEARL: There's been times we said no to what this patient asked for..

JEROME: You mean sleeping pills.

PEARL: Sleeping pills, scissors...

JEROME: This is more positive, Pearl

PEARL: I'll give you that.... What turned her around, you think? Just the boy?

JEROME: The boy. Or the new meds. Or the last shock treatment. Or none of the above. What a wonderfully precise profession we're in, Pearl! In scientific terms, there is no control.

(SKIP's voice is heard off.)

SKIP: (Off) Hello!

JEROME: (Checking watch; to PEARL) Right on time. (Calling back) We're back here, Skip!

PEARL: I'll round up Miss Massachusetts. (Starts out, stops) I sure hope this book of yours gets a happy ending.

JEROME: Let's try to give it one, Pearl.

(SKIP comes in. He is more dressed up for the occasion)

PEARL: *(Going to him)* I'm fetching your date, honey. *(She turns and goes.)*

SKIP: *(To* JEROME*)* My date?

JEROME: Mary thinks you're a gentleman caller.

SKIP: What is this? Tennessee Williams?

JEROME: Without the Southern accent.

SKIP: Don't tell me I have to put on an act?

JEROME: You may have to wing it a little.

SKIP: Boy.

JEROME: I thought you were good at playing by ear.

SKIP: According to my mother.

JEROME: I'm assuming you'll tell her about this.

SKIP: Depends what happens.

JEROME: Fair enough.

SKIP: Hey. Dig the flowers.

JEROME: Tell Mary you brought them.

SKIP: That feels phony.

JEROME: Up to you.

SKIP: I don't want any bullshit here.

JEROME: I understand.

SKIP: I came because she asked me.

JEROME: I understand.

SKIP: She's family, after all. It's kind of my responsibility.

JEROME: You sound like your mother.

SKIP: I know, goddammit. Will you be here to help me out?

JEROME: Sitting on the sidelines, taking notes.

SKIP: Notes? You're putting me under the gun.

JEROME: Just ignore me. *(Indicating his notebook)* It's just that there may be a hidden meaning here somewhere. It may all add up.

SKIP: You sound like my English professor....

JEROME: Not much difference between analyzing a poem and a person.

SKIP: Except the person is a human being.

JEROME: Good point.

(PEARL appears in the doorway.)

PEARL: Ta da.... *(Over her shoulder)* Come on in, Mary. *(Singing)* Here she is, Miss America!

(MARY appears on the landing. She looks younger, prettier, neater—and endearingly out of date. She wears something that looks vaguely like a prom dress and her hair is in the teased style of the Sixties. She comes down the stairs and stands shyly in the middle of the room)

PEARL: Say hello, Mary.

MARY: Hello.

JEROME: You have a visitor, Mary.

MARY: Who?

JEROME: Three guesses.

MARY: *(Seeing SKIP)* Oh, him.

SKIP: Hi, Mary.

MARY: Hello there. *(Noticing the flowers)* Did you bring me those ?

SKIP: No, I didn't.

MARY: Yes you did.

SKIP: They were here already.

MARY: I know you brought them. You're just being shy.

SKIP: *(With a glance at* JEROME*)* O K. I brought them.

MARY: Thank you. *(To* PEARL*)* What do I do now?

PEARL: What would you like to do, honey?

MARY: I'd like to talk. *(To* SKIP*)* Would you like to do that?

SKIP: Talk? Sure, Mary.

MARY: Let's sit down and make a conversation. *(Looks around)* Where should I sit? *(To* PEARL, *indicating the couch)* Should I sit there?

PEARL: Sit anywhere you want, child. You the boss.

MARY: *(Sitting)* All right. I'll sit here. And... *(Indicating a nearby chair to* SKIP*)* You sit over there, and... *(Indicating* JEROME *and* PEARL*)* You two can listen to our conversation while we're making it.

(Everyone sits.)

MARY: Good... Now let's start. *(To* SKIP*)* You first.

SKIP: *(Glancing for help from* PEARL *and* JEROME*)* It's... good to see you again, Mary.

MARY: I've been sick, you know. *(Indicating* JEROME*)* Ask him. He knows. I've been quite sick, haven't I?

JEROME *You have indeed, Mary.*

MARY: *(To* SKIP*)* Sometimes I've been confined to my room. *(Indicating* PEARL*)* But Kathleen here has been very good to me.

PEARL: Kathleen?

JEROME: *(Low to* PEARL*)* Stay with it.

MARY: Kathleen's from Ireland.

PEARL: That's a good one.

JEROME: (*Low to* PEARL) Kathleen must be a maid.

PEARL: (*Low to* JEROME) Wouldn't you know I'd end up playing the maid.... (*Trying an Irish accent*) Sure, and that's a good one, ma'am.

JEROME: (*Low to* PEARL) Not bad.

MARY: (*To* SKIP) Kathleen took good care of me when I was sick. She brought me food and drink. She helped me take a bath. Sometimes she took me out-of-doors for a breath of fresh air, didn't you, Kathleen?

PEARL: (*Irish*) Sure and I did, lass.

MARY: Remind me to remember you at Christmas time, Kathleen.

PEARL: That I will, ma'am. (*She sits down informally near them, then jumps up, remembering she's the maid*)

MARY (*To* SKIP) But I'm not sick now. I'm on the mend.

SKIP: Good for you, Mary.

MARY: Is that why you came to call?

SKIP: Right. To help you get better.

MARY: Have you been sick, too?

SKIP: Me? No. Not that I know of.

MARY: You look sick.

SKIP: Do I?

MARY: You look pale. Have they made you stay indoors?

SKIP: They have, Mary.

MARY: Have they made you work in the barn?

SKIP: The barn?

MARY: Or the stable? I'll bet they've made you shovel manure.

SKIP: They sure have. *(Low to others)* All term long.

MARY: You tell them you belong out of doors. Say you need sun and fresh air. Tell them to let you exercise the horses. Or work in the vegetable garden. *(To others)* He grows delicious tomatoes. He started the asparagus and put in the raspberries. We have white raspberries, too, and guess who put those in. If you serve them with our own fresh cream, they're the most delicious thing in the world. *(To SKIP)* Am I right?

SKIP: You are right, Mary. *(Low to JEROME)* She must be talking about Cooperstown.

MARY: *(Indicating SKIP)* This man plays the piano, too.

JEROME: *(Low to PEARL)* This is fascinating..

SKIP: I don't play the piano, Mary.

MARY: You're just saying that because you're shy with people who live in the big house. *(To others)* When you people are not here, he sneaks into the sunroom and plays the piano. And I don't mean *Chopsticks*, either. He plays *The Yellow Submarine.*

JEROME: Does he play *You are My Sunshine*, Mary?

MARY: Oh yes! Easily! I heard him playing that when I was sick! *(Sings)*
You are my sunshine, my only sunshine...
(To SKIP) You make music. You make things grow. You're good with animals. You are a Jack of all trades.

SKIP: *(To others)* And master of none.

(JEROME is writing away in his notebook.)

MARY: *(To PEARL)* Kathleen, perhaps this young man would like a glass of iced tea. Or even a glass of beer. *(To SKIP)* Do you like to drink beer?

SKIP: Actually I do.

MARY: Bring him beer, please, Kathleen.

(PEARL *hesitates.*)

But just ice-water from me. I'm not quite old enough yet for alcoholic beverages.

PEARL: Yes, ma'am.

JEROME: *(Low to* PEARL*)* There may be a beer in the guest fridge.

PEARL: Gotcha. *(She goes.)*

JEROME: *(As he writes; low to* SKIP*)* This is exciting. Keep it up.

MARY: *(To* JEROME*)* Excuse me.

JEROME: Yes, Mary?

MARY: May I be alone with my friend?

JEROME: Ah well...

SKIP: *(Low to* JEROME*)* I can deal with it.

JEROME: *(Low to* SKIP*)* I'll be right outside.

SKIP: O K...

JEROME: *(To* MARY*)* I'll go then, Mary. *(To both, pointedly)* I'm leaving the door open. *(He does. And goes)*

MARY: *(Confidingly)* They don't like us to be alone.

SKIP: I know.

MARY: Remember when they went on that picnic? And I couldn't go because I had broken my ankle playing Kick the Can? Remember that?

SKIP: I do.

MARY: They made Kathleen give up her whole day off to stay here with me. You know why?

SKIP: Why?

MARY: To keep me from seeing you.

SKIP: I didn't know that.

MARY: That's why they shipped me off to boarding school, too.

SKIP: Did they?

MARY: Oh yes. There's a perfectly decent school right here in Cooperstown, but they wanted to separate us, so they shipped me off.

SKIP: I see.

MARY: They found out about the boathouse, too.

SKIP: The boathouse.

MARY: Somebody noticed the mattress up in the loft. Somebody told. So now they know about that.

SKIP: Uh oh.

MARY: You can say that again. *(Pause)* Say it again.

SKIP: Uh oh.

MARY: Exactly! That's why they made you leave, isn't it? Because of what we did in the boathouse.

SKIP: I guess it was.

MARY: Why did you come back?

SKIP: You mean now?

MARY: Yes. Why are you here now?

SKIP: To see you, Mary.

MARY: Really?

SKIP: Really.

MARY: Are you glad you came?

SKIP: I am. Very much so.

MARY: They say you're bad for me. They say you're just out to get my money.

SKIP: Who says that?

MARY: The family says it. Are you out to get my money?

SKIP: No, Mary. Not me.

MARY: I think you're good for me.

SKIP: I hope I am.

MARY: In fact, if you weren't here, I don't know what I'd do.

(PEARL *comes in, carrying a can of beer and glass of water*)

PEARL: *(Handing them out; still Irish))* Here we are: water...and beer.

MARY: *(Haughtily)* We use trays in this house, Kathleen.

(PEARL *is stopped in her tracks*)

MARY: And we put beer in glasses. Remember that next time, please.

PEARL: I will; Miss. *(She starts to sit in her former place.)*

MARY: That will be all, Kathleen.

PEARL: Oh but...

SKIP: *(Opening his beer)* It's O K, Kathleen.

PEARL: Ah. Then I'll be going about me business. *(She goes out muttering)* Hoity-toity-toity

MARY: *(To* SKIP*)* What have you been doing?

SKIP: Me?

MARY: Since you left Cooperstown.

SKIP: Oh. Well...

MARY: Have you been working?

SKIP: Trying to.

MARY: Do you like your work?

SKIP: Not the way I should.

MARY: Would you prefer to be here?

SKIP: Here?

MARY: Working on the farm.

SKIP: I'd like that.

MARY: Trouble is, they'll send you away again. Have you thought of going somewhere else to do what you want to do?

SKIP: I have. Many times.

MARY: Could I go with you?

SKIP: What?

MARY: When you go, would you take me with you?

SKIP: Um...

MARY: I'll go with you anywhere. Anywhere you want to take me. Where shall we go?

SKIP: Um...

(JEROME *enters.*)

JJEROME: I think maybe we've had enough for one day.

MARY: *(Low to* SKIP*)* Uh oh. They're back from their picnic.

SKIP: Looks that way.

MARY: *(To* JEROME*)* We've been having our own picnic right here.

JEROME: Good for you, Mary.

MARY: But please, please, may we have a few minutes more, please? He's telling me what he wants to do in life.

JEROME: All right, Mary. A few more minutes.
(He withdraws.)

MARY: *(Suddenly, frantically)* Let's leave right now.

SKIP: Now?

MARY: *(Going toward the French doors)* Let's sneak out
quickly, the back way. I'm not happy here.

SKIP: Mary...

MARY: I'm serious. Let's vamoose! Let's go on the lam!
My Daddy left me lots of money. I'm loaded. We can
do whatever we want..

SKIP: Thanks, Mary, but I'm tied up at the moment.

MARY: You don't look tied up.

SKIP: It's just an expression, Mary. It means I have other
obligations.

MARY: Obligations?

SKIP: Things people want me to do..

MARY: Do you have another girl?

SKIP: *(After a pause)* I do.

MARY: Do you love her?

SKIP: *(Another pause)* No.

MARY: But she's an obligation.

SKIP: One of many, Mary.

MARY: Do you want to get rid of these obligations?

SKIP: I'm trying.

MARY: While you try, can you still see me?

SKIP: Sure I can.

MARY: Because maybe I can help.

SKIP: Maybe you can, Mary.

MARY: And you can help me.

(SKIP *moves toward the door*)

MARY: Are you leaving now?

SKIP: I think I'd better.

MARY: Otherwise, they'd make you go. Right?

SKIP: Right, Mary.

MARY: Will you come back?

SKIP: I sure will.

MARY: Good. Because I don't think I could live without you. You're the light of my life.

SKIP: Oh Mary.

MARY: So come back soon please.

SKIP: I definitely will. (*He's almost at the door.*)

MARY: Hey!

SKIP: What?

MARY: Aren't you forgetting something?

SKIP: Such as what?

MARY: What you always do. (*Looks around*) When no one's around. (*Pause*) You kiss me, you silly billy.

(SKIP *glances toward the door, then goes to her, kisses her. She holds him. It turns into quite a kiss.*)

SKIP: Goodbye, Mary. (*He goes.* MARY *is alone on stage.*)

MARY: (*Singing, dancing around*)
You are my sunshine...my only sunshine...
You make me happy...

(PEARL *comes in.*)

PEARL: Have a nice visit, Mary?

MARY: Wonderful, wonderful, wonderful, wonderful.

(MARY *dances around the room as* JEROME *comes in.*)

PEARL: *(Aside to* JEROME*)* She's repeating.

JEROME: *(Aside to* PEARL*)* We all do that when we're happy.

PEARL: *(Taking her arm)* Come on upstairs, Mary honey.

(They start for the stairs. Then MARY *stops, suddenly all business.)*

MARY: Do you drive a car, Kathleen?

PEARL: *(Irish accent again)* Sure and I can, ma'am. Would you like me to take you out in the car sometime?

MARY: Take me out right now, Kathleen. We need to go shopping.

PEARL: Shopping, ma'am?

MARY: I don't like what I'm wearing. It seems sort of...old-fashioned, Kathleen.,

JEROME: *(To himself; frantically writing)* More and more interesting.

*(MARY *hurries to the bookcase, looks through a stack of old* New Yorker *magazines.)*

MARY: I know you worked hard on this dress, Kathleen, but what I want to wear is... *(Finds the copy she's looking for)* Something more like... *(Shuffles through the magazine)* This. Right here. *(Shows* JEROME *and* PEARL *an ad)* Can we find something like this, Kathleen?

JEROME: *(Low to* PEARL*)* Try the Chestnut Hill Mall.

PEARL: *(Low to* JEROME*)* Now?

JEROME: *(Low to* PEARL*)* While iron is hot. *(Takes a credit car from his wallet)* Here's the institute card.

MARY: *(Now on the landing; to* JEROME*)* What does the word "splurge" mean?

JEROME: It means to throw money around.

MARY: That's what I thought. Come on, Kathleen. We're going to splurge. *(She goes out imperiously.)*

*(*JEROME *and* PEARL *linger briefly.)*

JEROME: We're headed into uncharted territory here.

PEARL: I'm scared. Are you?

JEROME: I am.

PEARL: You better call the mama.

JEROME: Not yet.

PEARL: Why not?

JEROME: That's really what scares me.

*(*PEARL *hurries off upstairs.* JEROME *writes in his notebook The sextet from* Lucia di Lammermoor*comes on.)*

(Slow blackout)

END OF ACT ONE

ACT TWO

(A few weeks later. :Possibly more music from Lucia di Lammermoor. *Voices out in the hallway.* LYDIA *comes on, followed by* JEROME; *they are talking as They enter.* JEROME *might wear a different, lighter jacket.* LYDIA *wears spring clothes.)*

LYDIA: I... Am... Flabbergasted!

JEROME: As are we all.

LYDIA: When you called, I almost flipped my lid.

JEROME: I can imagine.

LYDIA: The fact they even connected is one thing, but to hear that it's gone on from there! And all within a period of...how long since I was here?

JEROME: Six weeks.

LYDIA: This is one for the books!

JEROME: Does it disturb you?

LYDIA: Dis*turb* me? No! Of course not! I think it's wonderful! Except Skip might have let me know.

JEROME: I understand.

LYDIA: Not that he's ever been a well of information... And you say he's the one who's been calling the shots?

JEROME: It would seem so.

LYDIA: I stand amazed! I mean, Skip was won the leadership prize at Andover, but I never knew he could cast out devils.

JEROME: Ah well. It's partly Mary, too, of course.

LYDIA: I should hope so.

JEROME: And it could also be the new drug....

LYDIA: Next thing we know, we'll be reading about this in *The New York Times.*

JEROME: Or in a book.

LYDIA: A book? You think?

JEROME: Actually, I'm writing one.

LYDIA: On this?

JEROME: *(Patting his folders)* Are you comfortable with that?

LYDIA: Not if you mention our names.

JEROME: I don't have to.

LYDIA: I want you not to.

JEROME: Anonymous it will be.

LYDIA: I'm thinking of Skip, of course. His friends at Harvard would tease him mercilessly if they read he had spent his spring performing miracles.

JEROME: I understand.

LYDIA: Of course, his professors might give him extra credit.

JEROME: Why not?

LYDIA: Where is he now, by the way?

JEROME: I sent them out so we could catch up.

LYDIA: Them?

JEROME: He's with Mary.

LYDIA: Oh right. Of course. ...Does he know you called me? Does he know I'm here?

JEROME: I told him.

LYDIA: What did he say?

JEROME: He said "Bring it on".

LYDIA: "Bring it on"? Good Lord! Isn't that what George Bush said when he went into Iraq?

JEROME: Skip was kidding, of course.

LYDIA: George Bush wasn't...Skip thinks I'm a meddling mother, Jerome... And maybe I am. And why? Because his father is wandering around the West Coast, fondling a saxophone, having washed his hands of any and all responsibility. So the mantle has fallen on *moi* ...Did you know that things have become even more precarious at Harvard?

JEROME: I'm sorry to hear that.

LYDIA: He's been cutting classes right and left. And failing several of his courses. Apparently there's now some question whether he can even return next year, let alone graduate. His girl keeps telephoning me.

JEROME: He hasn't mentioned his girl.

LYDIA: He probably feels guilty about her. She's been working overtime to keep him up to the mark. They met last year when they were both pre-meds. She got him through organic chemistry.

JEROME: She sounds like a winner.

LYDIA: And Jewish, you'll be glad to know.

JEROME: Why should I be glad?

LYDIA: Because you are yourself

JEROME: I am. Yes.

LYDIA: Well Becky is, too. Rebecca Seligman, from New York City. I tease him about her. I call her "Rebecca of York".

(JEROME *doesn't get it.*)

LYDIA: After the character in *Ivanhoe* by Sir Walter Scott?

(JEROME *still doesn't get it.*)

LYDIA: Elizabeth Taylor played her in the movie? She's much more appealing than the cold Saxon princess Ivanhoe is supposed to marry. I thought that being Jewish you might be up on that.

JEROME: I am now.

LYDIA: .Aaanyway, like most Jewish people, Becky knows where she's heading, and how much work it takes to get there. I keep hoping some of that will rub off on Skip. *(Checking her watch)* Did you tell him when I'd show up?

JEROME: I did. But he and Mary take their own sweet time.

LYDIA: Oh really?

JEROME: It's quite a relationship.

LYDIA: "Relationship." Everyone uses that word these days, and I'm never quite sure what it means.

JEROME: In this case, it means that they're very fond of each other.'

LYDIA: Why?

JEROME: Why are they fond of each other?

LYDIA: Well I mean...

JEROME: They seem to satisfy each other's needs.

LYDIA: Needs? Needs?

JEROME: He reminds her of someone she once knew and liked. And she makes him feel important and necessary.

LYDIA: He's important and necessary to me, sir.

JEROME: Of course, but in Mary's case, he feels he's accomplishing something. He's easing her back into the world.

LYDIA: While she's easing him out of it. Neglecting his girl. Cutting his classes...

JEROME: I'll remind him of his responsibilities.

LYDIA: As will I, dear Doctor. You can be sure of that. *(Looks at watch again; gets up impatiently)* What are they doing? Tip-toeing through the tulips? Let's go waylay them.

JEROME: I believe they're out in the car.

LYDIA: Car? What car? Skip can't afford a car.

JEROME: Mary can.

LYDIA: She's bought a car?

JEROME: Skip leased one for her. A snappy blue Beamer convertible.

LYDIA: Oh Lord.

JEROME: Mary likes the fresh air.

LYDIA: Don't tell me she's doing the driving.

JEROME: No, but Skip is a good driver.

LYDIA: You might have consulted the trustee on this one.

JEROME: I was sure you'd go along with it.

LYDIA: I suppose I have to, don't I? If it's making everyone so deliriously happy. Where do they drive?

JEROME: All over.

LYDIA: All over?

JEROME: He's been giving her the grand tour of the Boston area. Let's see. They've been down to the Plymouth Plantation and up to Salem and out to Concord and the rude bridge that arches the flood. They've taken the Freedom Trail to the Old North Church. Skip is walking Mary through a refresher course in early American history.

LYDIA: And she gets it? She knows what's going on?

JEROME: Skip is very good at explaining things.

LYDIA: When he wants to be.

JEROME: He wants to be now. They also go hear a lot of music. She loves the Boston Symphony Orchestra.

LYDIA: How fancy. Has she got anything to wear? I mean, to a concert in town?

JEROME: Skip's taken her shopping.

LYDIA: Skip? Come on. He's hopeless on clothes.

JEROME: Mary isn't. And Pearl goes along to help.

LYDIA: Sounds like they're a ducky little trio.

JEROME: *(Patting his notes)* It's fun writing about.

LYDIA: Look, Jerome, I don't want to be a wet blanket, but has anyone bothered to think about what happens next? To Mary, I mean. Hopefully Skip can talk his way back into Harvard. And you and Pearl can go on working here. But what about Mary? What happens to her on down the line?

JEROME: They've been talking about that.

LYDIA: Oh they have, have they?

JEROME: Skip said they talked about it last Saturday. When they drove to Cooperstown.

LYDIA: What? They went to Cooperstown?

JEROME: She wanted to see her family's place.

LYDIA: It's all torn down. There's nothing there.

JEROME: The garden's there, they said. The town keeps it up.

LYDIA: That I didn't know.

JEROME: And Mary likes opera. So they stopped at the Glimmerglass opera house, and bought tickets for this summer.

LYDIA: Skip's got a job this summer. Back in Buffalo.

JEROME: He plans to take a weekend off to take Mary to the opera. They've already made reservations at some motel.

LYDIA: What kind of reservations?

JEROME: I don't know what kind, Lydia. I suppose the same kind they had this time.

LYDIA: What? They spent the night in Cooperstown?

JEROME: It's a long drive.

LYDIA: Well I mean did they have separate rooms?

JEROME: I didn't ask.

LYDIA: Don't you think you should?

JEROME: I have no intention of making an issue of it.

LYDIA: Oh yes? And what if they're sleeping together?

JEROME: Oh come on. She's twice his age.

LYDIA: I'm sorry. Skip can be very attractive. A woman in my book club saw him during our coffee break and started pawing him.

JEROME: Skip and Mary have a sweet and constructive relationship.

LYDIA: All well and good, but. it sounds slightly...
what's that word everyone throws around these days?
...Slightly "inappropriate". Where are they now, for
example? In some motel?

JEROME: They're at the Isabella Stuart Gardiner
Museum, looking at Early Renaissance art.

LYDIA: Oh really. Well, let me tell you something,
Jerome. I don't believe in talking behind people's backs,
but it's time you learned a thing or two about our dear
Crazy Mary.

JEROME: I've read all her folders, Lydia.

LYDIA: You may know the psychological stuff, dear
Doctor, but I doubt if you know the cold, hard facts.
I happen to have done a little detective work back in
Buffalo. I paid a call on old Mrs Sidway who went to
Cooperstown every summer before they tucked her
away in a nursing home. She gave me the straight
scoop about Mary, in case you're interested.

JEROME: I'm interested in anything which will help....

LYDIA: Well here's the thing, my friend. Mary happens
to be the result of an affair between my grandfather's
brother and a woman who came in to do the ironing,
whenever she wasn't sleeping with everyone else
in town. And after Mary was born, Our Lady of the
Laundry got post-partum depression big time, and
jumped off the bridge at Seneca Falls. My great-uncle
was suddenly stuck with a baby girl he wasn't even
sure was his.

JEROME: All right, all right.

LYDIA: Oh but there's more. He was sportsman enough
to accept responsibility. And unattached enough to
make her his next of kin. And drunk enough, a year
or two later, to drive his car into a stone wall and get
himself killed. Which left little orphan Mary growing

up in Cooperstown, brought up by Irish maids and a German governess until she started sleeping with a farm boy who worked around the place. The family fired the boy, and threw Mary into a boarding school, until she started exhibiting the same mental problems as her mother. That was when they decided to ship her off to the fanciest sanitarium they could find, dragging her trust fund behind her.

JEROME: As the current head of that fancy sanitarium, let me say this, Lydia: from what I've seen of Mary these past few weeks, I'm beginning to think that if she'd been welcomed rather than dismissed by that family of hers, she might have become a contributing member of society.

LYDIA: All I know is that my only son, with his whole life ahead of him, seems to have become involved in a peculiar relationship which leads nowhere for both of them. So you'll forgive me, dear Doctor, if I gently lower the boom on the whole operation.

JEROME: Go easy now, Lydia.

LYDIA: Don't worry about that. I've learned to be tactful all my life.

(PEARL *pokes her head in the door.*)

PEARL: They're back.

JEROME: Tell Skip his mother is here, would you, Pearl?

PEARL: Sure an' begorra that I will. (*She goes.*)

LYDIA: What's with the accent?

JEROME: She's pretending she's Irish.

LYDIA: This is turning into an absolute madhouse!

JEROME: That's what it's supposed to be.

(SKIP *comes in, looking bright and happy.*)

SKIP: Hiya, Mom.

LYDIA: *(Kissing him)* Hello, darling

SKIP: Have a good flight?

LYDIA: What a ridiculous question! No one has a good flight these days. Flying is a disagreeable and degrading experience, unless you're a rich Republican riding around in a private plane.

SKIP: *(To* JEROME*)* She's in a pissy mood?

LYDIA: Not at all. Where's my dear cousin?

SKIP: Pearl's giving her her meds.

LYDIA: Sounds like she needs an extra dose.

SKIP: *(To* JEROME*)* Looks like my mother and I need to review the bidding.

JEROME: I'll go. *(He does.)*

LYDIA: I must say you look wonderful, sweetheart.

SKIP: Thanks.

LYDIA: No, I mean it, you do. I'm delighted you've taken advantage of the lovely spring weather.

SKIP: As opposed to huddling in the dank stacks of the Widener library, yes.

LYDIA: I hope you've been getting some exercise.

SKIP: Oh sure.

LYDIA: Have you? Sitting in a convertible? Or are you and Mary taking up tennis?

SKIP: You'll be glad to know, Mom, I'm still running my five point eight miles, two or three times a week, along the Charles River.

LYDIA: Does it help?

SKIP: Help what?

LYDIA: You used to say that running dispelled your anxiety.

SKIP: I sure feel less anxious. But not because of the running.

LYDIA: Oh I see. It's because you've been having a little fling .

SKIP: Here it comes.

LYDIA: No, really. It sounds like you're doing a very good deed.

SKIP: It's more than that.

LYDIA: Whatever it is, I think it's terrific.

SKIP: Now for the "but".

LYDIA: No "buts" about it. In fact, it occurs to me you might take it one step farther.

SKIP: One step farther?

LYDIA: You might consider approaching this as a kind of a project. For that psychology course you're taking. Or supposed to be taking.

SKIP: Ah.

LYDIA: You could write a report on the whole thing. How Mary was when you met her, how you've helped her, and what her prospects might be for the future. You could submit it for credit.

SKIP: To Harvard.

LYDIA: Yes to Harvard. Certainly to Harvard. Or are you now attending some community college?

SKIP: I'm not sure what I'm attending. But I'm learning something, I'll tell you that.

LYDIA: Well, darling, if the bills I pay mean anything at all, you are still enrolled at Harvard University. So why not submit a special term paper to justify why you've been cutting classes.

SKIP: Oh Mother.

LYDIA: I am absolutely serious. I've been talking to Becky who thinks—

SKIP: You called Becky?

LYDIA: Becky called me.

SKIP: Goddammit, I wish she'd lay off.

LYDIA: She's trying to help, Skip. She said you're on the brink of probation. But this could solve that, darling.

SKIP: I don't consider Mary some sort of case study.

LYDIA: What do you consider her, darling?

SKIP: A friend.

LYDIA: I see. A friend.

SKIP: And a kindred spirit.

LYDIA: Oh really? And what, pray tell, do you think you're accomplishing with this kindred spirit?

SKIP: Helping her get on her feet.

LYDIA: At the risk of ruining your life?

SKIP: Or saving it.

LYDIA: You don't care about an education now?

SKIP: I'm getting a good one right here.

LYDIA: With Mary?

SKIP: Through Mary. She gives everything a fresh meaning. Being with her is like waking up on a spring morning after a long sleep.

LYDIA: Oh Skip, you sound like some soap opera.

SKIP: Yeah well it's true. I'm beginning to look at the world in a whole new way! Before, I was just going through the motions. Now it all seems fresh and exciting.

LYDIA: You can't be serious.

SKIP: I am, Mother. Totally.

LYDIA: Then I'm totally at a loss. I don't know what to do.

SKIP: Don't do anything, Mom. Ever thought of that? Just go with the flow.

LYDIA: I hate that expression, "Go with the flow. Go with the flow." You're getting into something that will be agonizing to get out of.

(PEARL *appears at the top of the stairs.*)

PEARL: *(Irish accent)* Her ladyship is ready for company.

SKIP: One minute, Pearl. O K.

PEARL: *(Theatrically)* Very well, sir. We'll withdraw to the withdrawing room.. *(She withdraws.)*

LYDIA: This is an absolute nightmare! That nurse pretending to be Irish, Jerome totally disregarding any professional standards, you behaving like a rebellious teenager, and Mary—did you tell her I was coming?

SKIP: I told her you were a visitor.

LYDIA: She doesn't know I'm your mother?

SKIP: I don't think so.

LYDIA: It's time she did.

SKIP: Treat her gently, O K?

LYDIA: I wasn't born yesterday, Skip.

SKIP: No, but Mary was. *(A moment. Then he goes up the stairs, knocks on the door)* O K, Pearl!

(PEARL *and* MARY *come out. This time* MARY *looks terrific. She's had her hair done in a more contemporary fashion, and wears something stylish and expensive.* JEROME *comes in discreetly behind, folder in hand)*

MARY: Here I am, "ready to roll", as Skip keeps saying. I've popped the appropriate pills, and gotten all gussied up for a guest, and now I'm—what's your expression, Skip? — "Loaded for bear."

LYDIA: I suppose I'm the bear.

MARY: What? No you're not... Not at all... Now wait... Don't tell me... I do believe you're...Lydia!

LYDIA: Good for you, Mary!

MARY: It's all coming back, thanks to Skip here.... *(Going to her)* Lydia, Lydia, lovely Lydia... *(Kisses her affectionately; to others)* We knew each other, once upon a time! *(To* LYDIA*)* We're even related, aren't we? In some strange way.

LYDIA: We are second cousins, once removed, Mary.

MARY: Once removed, twice shy.

SKIP: That's a good one, Mary.

LYDIA: Is it?

MARY: Let me look at you, Lydia *(She looks.)* Oh my. The years have been kind to you, Lydia!

LYDIA: And to you, Mary.

MARY: Me? Oh I'm a mess and willing to admit it. Life has dealt me a number of bad blows. But I'm bouncing back, Lydia. Bouncing back. Am I right, Jerome?

JEROME: You are right, Mary.

MARY: But hey. This feels like an occasion. Let's all have a drink. *(To* PEARL*)* Kathleen, would you bring us all a nice cocktail?

PEARL: Sure and I'd like to, Madam, but...

(She looks at JEROME.*)*

JEROME: There's a bottle of sherry in the lower right hand drawer of my desk.

PEARL: I don't think Miss Mary—

MARY: Oh, just water for me, Kathleen. *(To* LYDIA*)* I'm on this peculiar medicine, so I never mix, never worry. *(To* PEARL*)* Now go, go, go. Get glasses from the cafeteria. And remember to use a tray.

PEARL: Yes, Miss. *(She exits into the hall.)*

MARY: *(To* LYDIA*)* Isn't she adorable?

LYDIA: She's very sweet, Mary.

MARY: And guess what? She's not really Irish at all. She just likes to pretend, and we all go along with it.

LYDIA: I see.

MARY: But let's sit down and relax. *(Pats a place on the couch)* You sit here, Lydia, next to me. So we can catch up... *(To* SKIP *and* JEROME*)* As for you gentlemen, sit anywhere you want. Or you can go play squash, if you want. *(To* LYDIA*)* Remember grandfather's own, private squash court?.

LYDIA: I remember all that, Mary.

*(*JEROME *and* SKIP *sit to one side.)*

MARY: But all that's gone, isn't it? So, Lydia, tell me: what have you been up to since? Have the gods been good to you, or not?

LYDIA: It's a long story, Mary.

MARY: Then you're like me, cousin! I have a long story, too. But I prefer to throw the past to the winds, and focus on the present.

LYDIA: *(Glancing at* SKIP*)* I'm more interested in the future, Mary.

MARY: Yes, but at least let's fill in the blanks, Lydia. Where do you live, for example?

LYDIA: Buffalo.

MARY: Buffalo! So you went back. And stayed.

LYDIA: I did.

MARY: Do you feel trapped in Buffalo?

LYDIA: I don't have time to feel trapped.

MARY: I felt trapped here, once upon a time. But you don't at all? Do you work? Or play?

LYDIA: I do both, actually.

MARY: Have you ever fallen in love?

LYDIA: Yes, I have, Mary.

MARY: So have I. And I call that play.

LYDIA: Then I got married.

MARY: I call that work.

LYDIA: Hard work, Mary. Too hard. I'm divorced now.

MARY: Then you're like me more and more. You're a woman who's finally found her freedom. Or do you have children?

LYDIA: Just one. A boy.

MARY: A boy. How nice.

LYDIA: He's a very nice boy. In fact, he's sitting right there.

(Pause)

MARY: No!

LYDIA: Yes.

MARY: Skip is your son?

LYDIA: He is, Mary.

MARY: You're teasing me. The way you used to in Cooperstown. Skip couldn't possibly be your son. He's too old and you're too young.

LYDIA: Thank you very much, but he's mine, aren't you, Skip?

SKIP: She's my Mom, Mary.

MARY: How lucky for both of you!

LYDIA: Thank you, Mary.

MARY: But now it's my turn to tell you something surprising, Lydia.

LYDIA: Go ahead.

MARY: Your son here has become something of a beau of mine.

LYDIA: Oh really?

MARY: We are what you'd call "an item". By that I mean we've been seeing a lot of each other lately, haven't we, Skip?

SKIP: We have.

MARY: Isn't life strange, Lydia? Doesn't fate play amazing tricks? *(To* JEROME*)* Here Lydia and I are cousins, and now I'm kicking up my heels with her only child! *(To* LYDIA*)* Except he's not a child to me, Lydia. To me, he is more of a teacher or guide. *(To* SKIP*)* What's that word they kept using at the Boston Museum of Fine Arts?

SKIP: Docent.

MARY: That's it.... Skip is my docent, Lydia. He is walking me through the museum of life.

LYDIA: I see.

MARY: And it's all the more interesting because he's such an attractive man. Or do you think I'm robbing the cradle, Lydia? Now be perfectly frank.

LYDIA: I think...I think—

(PEARL *enters carrying a plastic tray with glasses of sherry and water for* MARY.)

PEARL: *(Always the Irish accent)* Here we are, lads and ladies... A drop, on the house, for old times sake.... *(She passes the drinks around.)*

MARY: I hope you brought one for yourself, Kathleen.

PEARL: Indeed I did, ma'am. .

MARY: Good for you. *(To* LYDIA*)* We live in a democracy, Lydia, and I believe in treating the servants with care and consideration.

PEARL: Thank you, Missus

MARY: Now where were we?

JEROME: You were asking Lydia how she felt about your friendship with Skip.

LYDIA: *(Dryly)* Thank you, Jerome, for putting us back on course. I can see you're very good at group therapy.

JEROME: Which is what this is, actually.

LYDIA: Is it really? O K. I'll play that game. So the question was how do I feel? I'd like to know how Skip feels first?

SKIP: Me?

LYDIA: You, Skipper. I'd very much like to hear about your feelings at this point.

SKIP: I've already told you, Mom.

MARY: You did? What did you tell her, Skip? *(To* LYDIA*)* Sometimes a man says different things to his mother than what he says to his lady love. A woman can hear the most charming things from the man she loves, and then find out he's leading her down the garden path. *(To* LYDIA*)* Am I right, Lydia?

LYDIA: You are, Mary. And I'm concerned about that garden path. I'm concerned where it might end up.

MARY: So am I, I promise you.. *(Confidingly)* I don't tell this to everyone, but I've been left in the lurch before. It was an extremely painful experience. *(To* SKIP*)* So tell me, Skip. How do you feel about me?

LYDIA: So come on, Skip. Let's hear it.

SKIP: I feel good making you feel good, Mary.

MARY: Doesn't it work both ways?

SKIP: It sure does, Mary.

MARY: I should certainly hope so. *(To* LYDIA*)* No offense, Lydia, but your son was kind of a sad sack when we first met. And sort of a smarty-pants, too. I've kind of brought him around. So it's a two-way street, isn't, Skip.

SKIP: Definitely, Mary

MARY: Especially when we went to Cooperstown. Do you know about our trip Cooperstown, Lydia?

LYDIA: I've heard something about it, yes.

MARY: Oh we had a high old time. The house has long since gone, but you can still see the garden and the stone terrace, overlooking the lake. And Grandma and Grandpa are still there.

LYDIA: Mary, Grandpa and Grandma have been dead for many, many years. *(She glances at* JEROME.*)*

MARY: I know that, silly. I'm talking about the two pine trees, side by side, down by the lake. One was taller than the other. We used to call them "Grandma" and "Grandpa" because grandma was taller than gramps. You remember that, don't you, Lydia?

LYDIA: *(Quietly)* I do now.

MARY: Tell her about the farm, Skip.

LYDIA: What farm?

MARY: We saw this farm. And—oh, you tell her, Skip.

LYDIA: I'd like very much to hear about the farm..

JEROME: Go on. Skip. This is new to me.

SKIP: Oh we were just driving around....

MARY: And we saw this farm. With a "For Sale" sign on it. So we stopped in.

SKIP: *(Initially reluctant to get into it)* No one was there, though.

MARY: No but we got out of the car and looked around. It was an old farmhouse, and it had this barn, and this chicken coop, and you could tell they used to have cows.

SKIP: You couldn't tell how much land they had.

MARY: So we stopped by this real estate office in town. And this man said it had fifty-three acres....

SKIP: All open land, all pretty much all fenced in, with an excellent artesian well...

MARY: So we're thinking of buying it.

LYDIA: What? Buying it?

SKIP: Just thinking about it.

LYDIA: Buying it with what?

MARY: Money, Lydia. My money. You may not know this, but I'm sitting on a huge pile. And I might as well put it to use.

SKIP: *(Getting with it)* Actually, it looks like a good farm.

LYDIA: You know nothing about farms, Skip. You've never come near a farm in your life.

SKIP: I came near this one.

LYDIA: So now you want to quit college so you can milk cows?

SKIP: No, Mom. No. I could commute to Ithaca, and take courses at Cornell, and get my degree in agriculture.

MARY: Tell her the kind of farm you'd make it? What's that word you used?

SKIP: Organic. It would be an organic farm.

MARY: And I'd fix up the house, and you could advise me, Lydia, because I'm sure you've got excellent taste, which I don't, because I've been out of the running for years.. So you could come help me pick out pillows and—

LYDIA: Stop! Stop it right now! *(Standing up)* All right, Skip. I've heard your feelings. And Mary, I've certainly heard yours. Would you like to hear mine?

MARY: Yes, Lydia. Very much.

JEROME: *(Standing up)* I think maybe we've had enough feelings for one—

LYDIA: Oh no you don't! It's my turn now. And my feelings are that this is the most ridiculous thing I ever heard in my life!

SKIP: *(Standing up)* Cool it, Mom

MARY: *(Standing up)* Would you like another drink, Lydia? Kathleen, would you go get—

LYDIA: Support me on this, Jerome. Isn't this just about the stupidest idea in the world?

JEROME: Why don't we all sit back down and quietly try to—

LYDIA: No, I can't listen a minute longer. Skipper milking cows, while Mary is doing what? Churning butter? And I suppose you'd be sleeping together, too!

SKIP: Jesus, Mom!

LYDIA: Well, would you?

SKIP: *(Angrily)* Hey yeah, Mom! What a good idea! Never thought of that one!

MARY: *(To SKIP)* Would you like to sleep with me, Skip?

JEROME: Slow down, everyone. Slow down.

LYDIA: Nobody's sleeping with anyone, Mary! Not while I have anything to say about it.

SKIP: Maybe you have nothing to say about it, Mom. Ever think of that?

LYDIA: I am her guardian! I am responsible for her well-being!

MARY: I don't like shouting. *(To LYDIA)* Could you lower your voice, Lydia?

LYDIA: *(Quietly)* Certainly. I'd be glad to, Mary. I just want to say that I happen to be the trustee of that money you two are throwing around. And I veto any and all farms here and now!

MARY: Are you jealous, Lydia. Are you jealous of our farm?

LYDIA: *(Bordering on tears)* I am not jealous, Mary. And I'll tell you why. Because it's nothing but a dumb dream cooked up by a mixed up kid and a lecherous old lunatic! *(She storms out.)*

(Long pause)

MARY: She called me a lunatic.

SKIP: She's called me worse than that, many times.

JEROME: I'd better go after her. *(He hurries off.)*

PEARL: *(To* MARY*)* You all right, honey?

MARY: *(Gathering up the sherry glasses)* That'll be all, Kathleen. We're having a private conversation.

*(*PEARL *leaves reluctantly with the tray of used glasses.)*

MARY: *(Quietly)* Lunatic I can understand because I live in a loony bin. Old? Maybe, but I don't feel old, thanks to you, Skip.

SKIP: Good.

MARY: But what does "lecherous" mean?

SKIP: I don't know, Mary.

MARY: You do, too. What does it mean?

SKIP: It means..."eager for love.'"

MARY: Do you think I'm eager for love?

SKIP: I think we all are, Mary.

MARY: She was right about that one. I know what it means to be eager for love. Someone once said he loved me, and I was eager for love every minute of the day.

SKIP: We all get that way, Mary.

MARY: Now I'm eager again. But no one has said anything about love.

SKIP: *(After a pause)* I love you, Mary.

(She looks at him.)

MARY: Say that again.

SKIP: I love you.

MARY: Do you? How do I know? How do I know?

*(She rushes up the stairs, closing the door behind her.
SKIP stands there, looking after her. JEROME comes in.)*

JEROME: Your mother's gone back to her hotel.

SKIP: Good.

(PEARL comes in.)

PEARL: *(Looking around)* Where's my baby?

SKIP: She went up.

PEARL: I'd better— *(She starts off.)*

SKIP: Hold it. *(He brushes past PEARL and JEROME)*

JEROME: Where are you going?

SKIP: To be with Mary.

PEARL: It's against the rules to go up there.

SKIP: Fuck the rules!

JEROME: *(Holding him)* I wouldn't, Skip.

SKIP: You wouldn't, I would. *(He breaks loose, hurries up
the stairs)*

PEARL: *(Starting up the stairs; to JEROME)* Get the orderly!

JEROME: *(Starting off)* .Who's on duty today?

PEARL: Whoever! Get going. Doctor! Move it!

*(JEROME hurriedly exits down the hall as PEARL exits up the
stairs. Music.)*

(Blackout)

*(The next morning. Morning light. Bird sounds. LYDIA ,
in different clothes, comes on somewhat furtively with her
carry-ont bag, which she places by the door. She crosses the*

stage and fusses with the coffee maker. After a moment, the
door opens at the top of the stairs and PEARL *comes down.)*

PEARL: *(Coldly)* There's fresh coffee and bagels in the
staff cafeteria.

LYDIA: I'm not sure I can face the staff. I certainly can't
face a bagel.

PEARL: You're kind of early, you know. The custodian
shouldn't have let you in.

LYDIA: I told him I had to catch a plane.

PEARL: Is that your standard excuse?

LYDIA: This time it's true.

*(*PEARL *turns to go.)*

LYDIA: Pearl...

*(*PEARL *stops.)*

LYDIA: Are you angry at me?

PEARL: Uh huh.

LYDIA: I don't blame you.

PEARL: You said some hurtful things.

LYDIA: I know. I want to apologize to everyone in sight.
I've already apologized to the custodian.

PEARL: He told me.

LYDIA: And I hereby apologize to you. Where's Jerome?

PEARL: Coming in.

LYDIA: I'll apologize to him.

PEARL: How about Mary?

LYDIA: Of course! Whenever you say.

PEARL: And your son.

LYDIA: I can't reach him....

PEARL: He's in the cafeteria.

LYDIA: First I'd better gird up my loins. Isn't that from the Bible?

PEARL: Uh huh.

(LYDIA *makes a face from sipping cold coffee.*)

PEARL: Sure you don't want it fresh?

LYDIA: Nope This will do me good. My cup of wormwood and gall. That's the Bible, too, isn't it?

PEARL: Book of Jeremiah. (*She turns to go.*)

LYDIA: .Pearl. Wait. (*Putting her coffee down*) Do you have children?

PEARL: Oh yes.

LYDIA: Boys?

PEARL: Oh yes.

LYDIA: Do they give you trouble?

PEARL: Try girls some time.

LYDIA: I suppose you have someone staying with them now.

PEARL: My Mama comes when I'm with my other child.

LYDIA: You mean Mary.

PEARL: She's my baby. (*She starts out again.*)

LYDIA: May I go up and see her?

PEARL: No, ma'am.

LYDIA: Just for a minute.

PEARL: No visitors above the first floor.

LYDIA: Surely I'm a special case.

PEARL: She won't open her door. I can't even give her her meds.

LYDIA: Are you sure she's—well, there.

PEARL: Oh she's there, all right. She hollered at me. Never hollered before.

LYDIA: What did she holler?

PEARL: "Go away. I'm busy."

LYDIA: Doing what?

PEARL: She said "Thinking".

LYDIA: Thinking about how horrible I was? Suppose I wrote her a note. Saying I'm truly embarrassed and ashamed. You could slip it under her door. Would that do it, Pearl.?

PEARL: No.

LYDIA: Or flowers then? How about flowers? What if I dashed out and bought a huge bunch of spring flowers, and sent them up, note attached. Would flowers work, Pearl?

PEARL: Lady, I don't think so.

LYDIA: Oh God, I'm hopeless, aren't I, Pearl. Flowers and notes. I feel like I'm wearing white gloves and a little hat. People don't change, do they, Pearl?

PEARL: Mary's changed.

LYDIA: True enough. But me? I'll never be really different. Oh I tried, twenty years ago, back in Buffalo. I defied my parents and crossed Main Street. I bridged the cultural divide, and married into we called the "vibrant Polish community". And after years of fights and apologies and marriage counselors, where are we now? Living a continent apart. Me, frantically hanging onto my heritage. Him, pouring out his Slavic soul through that sweet, sad saxophone. And both of us ritually repeating the same old gripes every time we talk.

PEARL: Go easy now.

LYDIA: Do you have a husband, Pearl?

PEARL: Not now.

LYDIA: But you won't talk about it.

PEARL: I leave all that at the gate.

LYDIA: But have you changed? Over the years?

PEARL: Tell you this, sugar. I have a heritage too. And I know I'm changed from that.

(SKIP comes in, looking somewhat bedraggled.)

LYDIA: Well, well. Look what the cat dragged in.

SKIP: I heard your voice.

LYDIA: *(To PEARL)* They say that up in Alaska, Pearl, a baby seal recognizes his mother's voice out of thousands others.

SKIP: It's the other way around. The mother does the recognizing.

LYDIA: *(To PEARL)* See how smart he is. *(To SKIP)* It's true. I always recognize yours.

SKIP: I'm not sure you do.

LYDIA: I must say it's been sounding different recently.

PEARL: I'll make another try with Mary's meds. *(She goes.)*

(Pause)

LYDIA: I tried to reach you last night. I was hoping we could at least break bread together.

SKIP: I haven't checked my cell.

LYDIA: Becky hasn't seen you all weekend.

SKIP: When will you two stop ganging up on me?

LYDIA: We love you. And we had no idea where you were.

SKIP: I was here. I spent the night with Mary.

LYDIA: Does Jerome know that?

SKIP: I don't think so.

LYDIA: That man is totally irresponsible.

SKIP: Not at all, Mom. Earlier in the evening he had me politely escorted downstairs by an orderly who applied a brutal half-nelson. But I found a way back..

LYDIA: Oh Skip. I have to say...I have to say...

SKIP: Mom, when will you learn you don't have to say anything?

(MARY *appears at the top of the stairs. She wears a tasteful new robe with silk pajamas underneath)*

MARY: Good morning.

LYDIA: Good morning, Mary.

MARY: *(To* LYDIA*)* Is he telling you I was lecherous last night?

LYDIA: Oh please, Mary. I apologize for that. I spoke in anger.

MARY: But you were right. I was very lecherous.

SKIP: You were not.

MARY: When Skip came to my room, I said, Stay with me, please. And when they dragged him away, I started screaming, didn't I, Skip?

SKIP: There was a lot of noise all around..

MARY: But then he sneaked up the fire-escape. Didn't you, Skip?

SKIP: I did.

MARY: And he was very polite. He knocked on my door. And then we both got really lecherous.

LYDIA: May we change the subject, please?

MARY: No, wait. In the morning, I asked him to go, Lydia..

SKIP: You sure did.

MARY: "O K, buster," I said. "Time to get up and get out." I kicked him out of bed. Literally. He fell flat on his bum.

SKIP: I did actually.

MARY: It was almost funny.

SKIP: Not to me.

MARY: I called him a kid, just as you did, Lydia. I said, "You're a good kid if you like kids."

SKIP: That's what you said.

MARY: So he grabbed his clothes and ran.

SKIP: Not true. I put on my clothes and went quietly down to the cafeteria.

LYDIA: *(Walking away)* I'm sorry, you two, but I'm not terribly interested in these gory details.

MARY: I'm saying it again. Skip.

SKIP: Saying what?

MARY: Go.

SKIP: O K. If you want.

MARY: And .please don't come back..

SKIP: Until when?

MARY: Until never.

SKIP: What?

MARY: I don't want to see you any more.

SKIP: You're serious, Mary?

MARY: I am, Skip. All that's over now..

SKIP: Why?

MARY: Because I'm older now.

SKIP: Oh come on.

MARY: I'm older than your mother. Aren't I, Lydia?

LYDIA: You are, Mary.

MARY: And I've lived more, haven't I, Lydia?

LYDIA: You have, Mary. In some ways.

MARY: I'm older, and wiser, and I can see around the corner. That's why I want him to go.

LYDIA: Good for you, Mary.

SKIP: Mary...

MARY: No, now go. Please. *(Holds out her hand)* Thank you very much for a lovely time..

SKIP: Mary...

MARY: No. Goodbye, Skip

SKIP: *(Hurt)* Goodbye.

(He shakes her hand quickly and hurries out.)

(Pause)

MARY: *(To* LYDIA*)* That was for you, Lydia.

LYDIA: Me? Well I do think it's best, Mary..

MARY: He's a good boy, though.

LYDIA: That I know.

MARY: Last night he was very sweet, and very tender, oh, and a very good lover.

LYDIA: That's enough, Mary.

MARY: *(Looking where* SKIP *has gone)* Do you think
I hurt his feelings?

LYDIA: He'll get over it. You hurt Pearl's feelings.
I'll say that....

MARY: Did Pearl want to sleep with me, too?

LYDIA: She wants you to take your pills.

MARY: Pills can be wrong. They make you think things
are fine when they're not at all. I'm trying to think
without pills. I'm trying to stop being a lecherous old
lunatic. That's why I gave him the old heave-ho. I did
it to get in your good graces. Are you proud of me?

LYDIA: Actually I am, Mary.

MARY: Trouble is, what do I do next?

(They sit side by side on the couch.)

LYDIA: I'll tell you exactly what, Mary. You continue
to make an effort. Jerome will help you, of course.
And Pearl will be right at your side. And maybe,
before long, we'll put our heads together and find
you a half-way house so you can connect with the
outside world.

MARY: How do I do that?

LYDIA: By meeting people, making friends.

MARY: I've got a lot of money. Will that help?

LYDIA: It sure will,, Mary. You'll be surprised.

MARY: Yes, but what will I do? Be specific.

LYDIA: Well, let's see. Boston is a wonderful town.
It has lots of things going on. Music, for example.
I'll personally see that you get a subscription to the
Boston Symphony Orchestra.

MARY: Who would take me? I won't have Skip any more.

LYDIA: We'll find a companion for you, Mary.
We might hire Pearl.

MARY: Eight hours a day of me is enough, Pearl says.

LYDIA: Then we'll find someone else.

MARY: *(Edging closer to* LYDIA *on the couch)* You could take me.

LYDIA: Me? Well of course, Mary. Whenever I'm here, we'll go to a concert.

MARY: Because you're beginning to like me, aren't you?

LYDIA: I like you very much.

MARY: I knew you'd like me if I sent Skip away. I knew you'd take me under your wing.

LYDIA: Whenever I'm here.

MARY: Would you take me to Buffalo?

LYDIA: Oh well. Buffalo....

MARY: I remember in Cooperstown everyone talked about Buffalo. The parties, the skiing, the fun...

LYDIA: All that's pretty much over.

MARY: But you like it there?

LYDIA: It's my home.

MARY: Then it's my home, too, isn't it? My grandfather came from there. So you could take me there. You could keep me from turning into a lecherous old lunatic.

LYDIA: Stop that, Mary.

MARY: You could help me make friends. You could give me a party, to get me started. You could help me buy a dress and teach me to make casual conversation. And I want to live in a carriage house. Like where I lived in Cooperstown. They put me in the carriage house with the chauffeur and the cook.

LYDIA: There are no carriage houses any more, Mary.

MARY: Then I'll stay with you.

LYDIA: Oh, Mary. I live in a small apartment....

MARY: Then we'll buy a house. With a garden and a pool. Because I'm loaded, Lydia. We'll buy a piano so we can all sing songs. You could tell people you're my guardian and I've landed in your lap. And if I start behaving like a lunatic, I'll try to warn you ahead of time, so you can give me my meds.

LYDIA: Mary, please listen...

MARY: Oh but one thing when I'm there: please ask people to talk slowly. Because lots of times, I can't understand a word they're saying. Even with Skip. Everyone speaks so fast these days. And they use strange words. I have to say "what?" all the time.

LYDIA: I haven't noticed you saying that, Mary.

MARY: What?

LYDIA: Now you're teasing me.

MARY: What?

LYDIA: No now look, Mary, here's the thing. I'm going to be very frank with you now. In some ways, you and I are both in the same boat. We're both leftovers from another way of life. People look at us and wonder "what old steamer trunk did she crawl out of."

MARY: That's funny.

LYDIA: And I say "what?" a lot, too. Sometimes I feel totally out of the loop..

MARY: What?

LYDIA: No, now cut it out, please. I'm serious now. You wouldn't be happy in Buffalo, Mary.

MARY: I would, I would.

LYDIA: No, no. Because we've sort of put our wagons in a circle back there. We've turned into a small, tight town,

MARY: I don't like big cities.

LYDIA: No, but listen. I'm smaller, too, Mary. I realize that now. I'm bossy. And mean and petty. And very set in my ways.

MARY: Me, too. Me, too.

LYDIA: No, it's not the same thing. Now maybe you could come to Buffalo for a weekend or something. But...

MARY: You don't want me there, do you?

LYDIA: Oh dear.

MARY: You don't want to take me on.

LYDIA: You'll be happier here, Mary.

MARY: You're going to leave me here?

LYDIA: Only until we find...until you find...only because...

(A moment)

MARY: Do you have a lover in Buffalo?

MARY: No..

MARY: I had a lover in Cooperstown.

LYDIA: I know you did, Mary.

MARY: A young lover.

LYDIA: I know that.

MARY: I've had one here, too.

LYDIA: Yes.

MARY: I've had young lovers twice in my life. I've been very lucky in that department.

LYDIA: Yes you have, Mary..

MARY: Maybe that's all I can ask for. *(She goes back upstairs, singing quietly.)* You are my sunshine, my only sunshine...

(LYDIA stands looking after her.)

(JEROME comes in)

JEROME: *(Looking after MARY)* Is she up or down?

LYDIA: I'm not sure..

JEROME: Skip's waiting by the front door. He wants to drive you to the airport.

LYDIA: Is that good or bad?

JEROME: Both I think.

LYDIA: *(Shaking hands with him)* Goodbye then, Jerome. Good luck with your book.

JEROME: I 'm calling it *Recalled to Life.*

LYDIA: I hope that means it has a happy ending.

(LYDIA goes. JEROME looks after her, then exits.)

(Music. A light change to late afternoon)

(Almost immediately .PEARL comes in, now wearing a more formal outfit.. She carries a large vase of lilies decorated with a large black bow. She sets it on a table as JEROME comes in, wearing a dark jacket and tie. He carries a tray containing a stack of plastic glasses and a couple of bottles of white wine.)

JEROME *(Setting up wine and glasses)* What's the count?

PEARL: Around a dozen, more or less. Consuella and Janice from the kitchen. Several of the nursing staff. Nick the gardener. Paul Elston from accounting, Kevin from Security. Mr. Devita, and some others from the group. And you and me.

(They organize the folding chairs into a couple of informal rows.)

JEROME: I located Skip. He's coming.

PEARL: Had he heard?

JEROME: I had to tell him.

PEARL: Poor kid.

JEROME: Well he's young,

PEARL: Consuella's made a food platter.

JEROME: Mary loved her quesadillas..

PEARL: Consuella loved Mary. *(She adjust the flowers)* These are from guess who. *(Reading the attached card)* "I am totally devastated" ...So devastated she couldn't make it..

JEROME: Yes well, I told her on the phone it was primarily an in-house thing.

(They continue arranging the chairs.)

PEARL: I still think Mary was off her meds. I think she flushed them down the toilet.

JEROME: We'll never know.

PEARL: She was doing fine. She had her T V hooked up. She asked me to teach her to drive.

JEROME: She certainly was involved in the therapy group. She even struck up a friendship with Mister De Vita.

PEARL: She told me.

JEROME: She went out for coffee with him. Twice. Which is why I signed her up for the group home.

PEARL: Do you think that's why she sneaked up to the old East Wing? Maybe she wanted to see where she was going. Maybe she climbed out on the roof for a better view.

JEROME: I've thought of that... A rainy night...a slippery slate roof... Maybe... Except her mother jumped, too.

PEARL: You think it was genetic?

JEROME: I think maybe, maybe, maybe, all the time....

PEARL: I should have locked that door to the East Wing.

(SKIP *comes in. He might wear a loose jacket and tie.*)

SKIP: And I should have at least come back for a visit.

(*Hugs* JEROME *and* PEARL)

JEROME: Woulda, shoulda, coulda. What is this? A guilt trip or a memorial service?

SKIP: (*Noticing the flowers*) I take it my mother's not coming.

JEROME: Couldn't make it. Would you like to say a few words?

SKIP: No.

PEARL: How about playing the piano?

SKIP: I'll do that.

JEROME: Maybe a hymn?

SKIP: *You Are My Sunshine.*

JEROME: Fair enough.

PEARL: I'm reading from the Bible.

JEROME: The thing to remember is that no one's to blame. Or everyone is.

SKIP: Do you say that in your book?

JEROME: My poor book. It doesn't even have a title now.

(LYDIA's *voice is heard calling from off.*)

LYDIA: *(Off)* Hello!

PEARL: Speak of the Devil.

JEROME: Easy now.

(LYDIA *hurries on, wearing something very stylish and black.*)

LYDIA: Am I too late? *(Looks around)* I take it I'm not. *(She shakes hands and gives a polite kiss to* JEROME. *She looks at the flowers)* Flowers aren't enough, are they, Pearl? *(She kisses* PEARL.*)*

SKIP: I thought you chickened out.

LYDIA: I did. *(Kissing him)* And changed my mind.

SKIP: Oh right. People do that, don't they? When they get rich.

JEROME: Let's settle down here, folks.

LYDIA: I wonder if I might have a brief moment alone with my son. Whom I haven't seen in several centuries.

JEROME: Pearl and I will round up the troops.

(JEROME *and* PEARL *go, closing the door behind them.*)

LYDIA: Becky tells me you've moved out.

SKIP: I got a six week gig up in New Hampshire. Clearing trails around Crawford notch...

LYDIA: How...enterprising.

SKIP: At least I did some thinking.

LYDIA: And where are you staying now?

SKIP: On Dickie Soule's couch.

LYDIA: Becky said her family will be skiing at Vail over Christmas, and you're welcome to come.

SKIP: No thanks.

LYDIA: Harvard is calling this whole thing a leave of absence.

SKIP: They can call it whatever they want. Me, I call it the Huck Finn option....

LYDIA: Which means?

SKIP: I plan to light out for the territory. Play some tunes with Dad. Look for a job.

LYDIA: Don't tell me farming?

SKIP: Whatever. I want to start from scratch, the way my great grandfather did.

LYDIA: And nothing I can say or do...?

SKIP: Nothing.

LYDIA: At least take my Toyota.

SKIP: What'll you drive?

LYDIA: I've ordered a new Lexus. Which will be waiting when I get back from Paris.

SKIP: Paris?

LYDIA: I haven't seen it since my junior year abroad. We're flying First Class and staying at the Ritz.

SKIP: We?

LYDIA: Me...and Diego...

SKIP: Crossing Main Street again, Mom?

LYDIA: I've known him for years. He's a first-rate contractor who renovates old houses. Maybe he'll renovate me.

SKIP: Have fun.

LYDIA: You know what will happen, don't you? It will rain, and we'll both catch colds. He won't appreciate the food, and we'll have a major argument in the

middle of some museum. And when I get back,
the Lexus will turn out to be a lemon.

SKIP: You sound a little guilty, Mom.

(JEROME *comes back in.*)

JEROME: Ready to start?

LYDIA: I want to say a few words. Since Mary was my
cousin.

SKIP: Once removed, and then returned to the library.
Like an unread book.

LYDIA: Oh Skip, please! Give me a break. (*To* JEROME)
I'll be very brief. I'll simply say I'm very appreciative of
how all of you here have treated Mary over the years.

JEROME: That would be nice, Lydia.

LYDIA: I might add that I grew up with her over the
summers in Cooperstown and how sweet she was
there, even when we teased her. And I'll say I'm sorry
I barged in here, and stirred things up, and...and then...
when she needed me, I didn't... I couldn't ... And how
I'd give anything in the world just to... Just to... Oh
dear. (*She turns away.*)

(PEARL *opens the door.*)

PEARL: The natives are restless.

JEROME: (*Indicating* LYDIA) A couple more minutes.

LYDIA: (*Pulling herself together*) And I'd like to say
something about the money.

JEROME: No need, no need.

LYDIA: No, I've been thinking about this. I want to say
I'm establishing a small endowment in Mary's name.

JEROME: That would be very generous, Lydia...

LYDIA: A small endowment. Except that sounds...what?

SKIP: That sounds small, Mom.

LYDIA: It does, doesn't it? All right, I'll say a substantial endowment. How about that? Oh hell, maybe I'll say I'm returning the whole damn thing! Except then I'll have to follow through, won't I?

SKIP: Yes, you will, Mom.

LYDIA: What if I say I'm returning *almost* the whole damn thing?

JEROME: Up to you, Lydia.

LYDIA: O K. I'll say that.

SKIP: Yes!

LYDIA: Now Jerome: I want to shake hands with people as they come in. Please stand beside me, and introduce them to me.

SKIP: Hey Mom. Hello. This isn't your wedding reception.

LYDIA: No it isn't, Skip. It's Mary's funeral service. And I'm a member of her family.

JEROME: You are indeed, Lydia.

(PEARL *appears in the doorway*)

PEARL: All set?

JEROME: As much as we'll ever be.

(SKIP *goes to the piano*)

LYDIA: (*To* JEROME, *as they go to stand by the door*) And I want to know everyone's name and what they do.

PEARL: (*Calling off*) Come on in, folks.

(SKIP *begins to play a slow version of* You Are My Sunshine.)

(LYDIA *stands between* PEARL *and* JEROME *as the lights focus in on them, waiting to meet the funeral guests. Fade to black.*)

(*Curtain*)

END OF PLAY

BACKGROUND MATERIAL

(Dates simplified and approximate)

LYDIA: (Born 1955—)

LYDIA's great-grandfather (born 1860, died 1940) built Mohegan Manor on Lake Otsego at Cooperstown. Had two sons: LYDIA's grandfather (1895-1975) and MARY's father (1900-1958).

LYDIA's grandparents hold onto the house, finally sell it in the Seventies.

LYDIA's father (1930-2007) becomes a negligent trustee.

LYDIA spends summers in Cooperstown during the Sixties; marries 1985; divorces in mid-Nineties.

SKIP (Born late 1980s)

Due to graduate from Harvard, June 2008.

MARY (1950-2007)

MARY's mother dies in the early Fifties

MARY's father (LYDIA's great-uncle) dies in an automobile accident in 1958.

MARY lives in Cooperstown winters and summers. Goes to boarding school during the late Sixties. Is committed to the Peabody Institute in 1973.

THE PEABODY FAMILY

Sells their estate on the North Shore of Boston during
the Depression. It becomes the Peabody Institute,
a private sanitarium.

www.ingramcontent.com/pod-product-compliance
Lightning Source LLC
Chambersburg PA
CBHW052157090426
42741CB00010B/2314